AN INDIAN TABLE

Shehzad Husain was born in Karachi where she spent her early childhood. She has written one other cookery book, *Entertaining Indian Style*, has contributed articles to various magazines and works as a consultant to a leading high street chain, advising them on their range of Indian food.

BY THE SAME AUTHOR

Entertaining Indian-Style

AN INDIAN TABLE

SHEHZAD HUSAIN

BRACKEN

This 1994 edition distributed by Bracken Books,
an imprint of Studio Editions Ltd.,
Princess House, 50 Eastcastle Street,
London W1N 7AP, England

Produced by arrangement with Carlton Books Limited.

First published in 1991 by
PAPERMAC
Cavaye Place, London SW10 9PG
and Basingstoke

ISBN 1-85891-335-7

Printed and bound in Great Britain by Mackays, Chatham

*With all my love to my husband Arif
and my three lovely children,
Humaira, Sumra and Asim,
may God bless them.
Amen.*

Bismillah – hir – Rahmaan – hir – Raheen
(in the name of Allah the beneficent, the merciful)

CONTENTS

ACKNOWLEDGEMENT

My special thanks to Mummy, who has been a constant source of support and encouragement.

INTRODUCTION

This simple, practical guide to Indian vegetarian and fish cookery was written because of the growing awareness of the need for a healthier diet. Although we are a Muslim family, and Muslims eat meat (except for pork), I have for many years been trying to encourage my children to cut down on meat for health reasons, and so I have included more and more vegetarian dishes on the menu at home. Their growing appreciation of the vegetable dishes that can be cooked in many delicious and varied ways encouraged me to compile this book.

The West has, in recent years, shown a keen interest in Indian culture and cuisine, and many people are now accustomed to eating Indian vegetarian food in Indian restaurants. I strongly believe, however, that you cannot beat good home cooking. My mother taught me to cook after we came to England from Hyderabad, when I was twelve and showing a keen interest in cooking, and she made me responsible for Sunday lunch. Hyderabad, in southern India, was founded in the sixteenth century and was one of the few states that boasted its own king. Its people are known for their insistence on etiquette and politeness (particularly towards their elders) as well as for their delicious and distinctive cuisine.

The recipes I have chosen for this book originate from all parts of India, but particularly from my home state. The Hyderabadis are famous for their biryanis, which are cooked for weddings and other special occasions, and whether they include meat, chicken or vegetables the end result is always delectable. Among their vegetarian dishes *Mirch Ka Salan* (green chilli curry, of which a milder version is achieved by using green pepper instead), *Bagare Baingun* (spiced aubergines) and *Aloo Methi* (potatoes with fenugreek) are some of the most mouthwatering. We Hyderabadis like our food to be tangy and spicy, so we use either tamarind or lemon to achieve this flavour. Though dishes like *Sambar* (lentils), *Idli* (steamed rice cakes) and

Masala Dosa (rice pancakes) all originated in the south, they are now eaten throughout India.

For religious reasons a great many people in India are vegetarians. Hinduism, India's indigenous religion for thousands of years, has had a profound influence on Indian cuisine. One of the central themes of Hinduism is the doctrine of Karma, the reincarnation of the soul. Hindus believe that after death the soul is reborn into this world but not necessarily in the human form, and whether one comes back as a human or an animal depends on one's conduct in this life. This principle, coupled with the idea of *Ahimsa* (non-violence to any creature) means that killing any animal for food is forbidden, and Hindus have mastered the art of vegetarian cooking through centuries of experiment. The cow is particularly venerated, so beef is strictly prohibited. These rules are followed with varying degrees of observance today, and the seafood and the vegan recipes included in this book reflect the broad range of modern Indian vegetarianism.

People who eat neither fish nor eggs make sure they have enough protein by eating the many different types of lentil (*dhaal*) available in India. Some thirty varieties of lentil are eaten, cooked in many different and interesting ways. When preparing an Indian vegetarian meal it is therefore always advisable to include a lentil dish, not only for the protein but because it will complement the majority of vegetable and rice dishes.

Indian vegetarian food is simple and quick to prepare, unlike meat dishes which take much longer to cook. Likewise fish and seafood dishes, using cooked frozen prawns and the wide variety of cleaned fresh fish now available in most supermarkets, are very easy and quick to cook. Fish is eaten widely all over the Indian sub-continent, and is best in Bangladesh where it is eaten mainly with rice.

Most Indian restaurants in Britain seem to offer very few desserts, even though a wide variety of delicious desserts is made in India. It may be that they are considered too sweet for the western palate, but I have included several in this book so that you can try them for yourself.

I have made a special effort to make the recipes in this book as straightforward as possible so that they give satisfying results every time. Though all the spices used in the recipes are carefully blended to complement and enhance the particular dish, cooking is an art and it is possible to add your own individual touch and change the flavourings to suit your own taste. Always taste as you cook for the best results.

If you are not familiar with Indian cuisine, read the introduction and method of the chosen recipe before you begin to cook, so that you make yourself familiar with the traditionally used techniques. Until recently, cookery books in India did not contain any precise quantities for ingredients and spices, since it was taken for granted that one would have a rough idea of how much to use. Freshly ground spices would always be used, but today ready-ground spices are also common in most Indian homes, and modern cooking utensils such as pressure cookers and food processors instead of the traditional pestle and mortar are also used as time-saving devices in the modern kitchen (see Equipment, below).

The recipes in this book have been chosen to reflect the wide variety of delicious Indian vegetarian dishes that are quick and easy to make. Even if you know nothing about Indian cooking, you will find that they are as enjoyable to prepare as to eat. Bon Appetit!

COOKING AND EATING VEGETARIAN FOOD

Equipment
You are likely to find that you already have all the equipment you need for cooking Indian food. Good-quality heavy-based saucepans and a frying pan, some wooden spatulas and, ideally, a slotted spoon for stirring rice are the first essentials. In an Indian kitchen you would probably find a *thawa*, which is a cast-iron frying pan used for cooking chapatis and paratas and for roasting spices; a *karahi*, a deep frying pan which resembles a straight-sided wok, made of aluminium or stainless steel, with handles on both sides; and possibly also a *girda*, a small (25cm/10 in in diameter) pastry board on short legs, used for rolling out dough. You will want at least one sharp knife and, for measuring, some spoons and a jug. Kitchen scales could be helpful, too.

For grinding spices you can use a pestle and mortar or pepper grinder, a coffee grinder or food processor, or even a rolling pin (you will need a rolling pin in any case for rolling out chapati and other dough). In many Indian households a flat, heavy grindstone and something like a rolling pin (called a *mussal*) are still considered the best solution. Some people find a garlic press useful too.

Electric rice cookers have become popular throughout the East, wherever rice is cooked regularly and in large quantities, because they ensure that the rice is always perfectly cooked and will stay warm until required, without burning.

Store cupboard items

Your basic stock of spices should include fresh ginger and garlic, chilli powder, turmeric, cardamom, black pepper, ground coriander and cumin. The powdered spices will keep very well in airtight containers, carefully labelled, while the fresh ginger and garlic will keep for seven to ten days in the refrigerator. Other useful items, to be acquired as your repertoire increases, are cumin seeds (black as well as white), onion seeds, mustard seeds, cloves, cinnamon, dried red chillis, fenugreek, vegetable ghee and garam masala (a mixture of spices that can either be bought ready made or home made in quantity for use whenever required).

PREPARATION TIPS

Using spices

It is always a good idea, particularly if you are not familiar with Indian cooking, to take out all the spices you need before you start cooking and keep them either on a plate or in small separate bowls. Chop onions and other vegetables also before you start.

There are many ways of using spices. You can use them whole, ground, roasted, fried or mixed. One spice can completely alter the flavour of a dish and different combinations of several can produce a variety of colours and textures.

Many of the recipes in this book call for ground spices, which are generally available in supermarkets as well as in Indian and Pakistani grocers. In India, we almost always buy whole spices and grind them ourselves, and there is no doubt that freshly ground spices make a noticeable difference to the end product. However, it is quicker and more convenient to use ground spices.

For some of the recipes the spices need to be roasted. In India this is done on a *thawa*, but a heavy, ideally cast iron frying pan may be used. No water or oil is added to the spices; they are simply dry roasted whole while the pan is shaken to stop them burning.

The quantity of spices shown in the recipes in this book are merely a guide. Do not hesitate to increase the quantities if you wish, especially in the cases of salt and chilli powder, which are very much a matter of individual taste and preference. Remember that long cooking over a lowish heat will always improve the taste of the food, as it allows the spices to be absorbed. This is why reheating a dish the following day is no problem with most Indian food. Do feel free to experiment with the different spices. The amount of chillies you use will decrease and increase the heat of your curry. Omit the seeds if you can't tolerate a very hot curry.

Ginger and garlic
As ginger and garlic are frequently used in curries, and it takes time and effort to peel and chop these every time, I suggest you take about 200g/8 oz of each, soak them overnight (this makes them easy to peel), peel and grind them separately, in a food processor, adding a little water to form a pulp. They can then be stored in an airtight container in a cool place for a month or even longer.

Yogurt
When adding yogurt to curries I always whip it first with a fork so that it does not curdle, and I add it gradually. Yogurt helps to tenderise meat and fish and give curry a thick, creamy texture. Always use natural unsweetened yogurt. *Raita*, yogurt sauce, also complements most curries beautifully.

The secret of a good curry
The final colour and texture of a curry depend on how well you browned the onions in the first stage. This requires patience, especially if you are cooking a large quantity. Heat the oil first, before you add the onions, then reduce the heat slightly so that the onions go golden brown without burning, and stir them gently with a wooden spoon or spatula.

Once this is done, add the spices, meat or other ingredients, as stipulated in the recipe, and mix and coat by *bhoono*-ing (stirring and frying in gentle semicircular movements, scraping the bottom of the pan). This is essential for a good end-result, and when you have done this you should taste the food and adjust the seasoning according to your own palate. Remember that the recipes are only guidelines, not prescriptions, so you do not have to follow them too rigidly.

Thickening sauces
In Indian cooking flour is seldom used to thicken sauces; instead, we rely on the onions and spices (such as ginger, garlic or powdered coriander) to produce a thick brown sauce.

Making a *baghaar* (seasoned oil dressing)
As far as I know this dressing is used only in Indian cooking. Oil or

ghee is heated to a very high temperature without burning, and spices, onions and herbs are dropped into the oil, immediately changing colour and becoming very aromatic; then the seasoned oil is removed from the heat and poured over the dish – cooked *dhaal* or vegetables, very often – like a dressing. Sometimes uncooked food is added to the heated oil, too, to be sautéd or simmered.

You will find full instructions for *baghaar* in the recipes, wherever they are required.

Freezing Indian food
The good thing about Indian food is that the majority of it can easily be frozen, with very little loss of flavour. The potato is an exception, though, as it becomes mushy when cooked and frozen in a curry. If you are going to cook and freeze a dish with potato, leave out the potato and add it on the day you are going to serve it.

To reheat on the day, defrost at room temperature for a few hours and then either place the item in the oven, in a saucepan or under a low grill as appropriate; you could also shallow fry, but I find this makes the food a little too greasy. A microwave oven is of course the latest answer to thawing and reheating frozen dishes.

PRESENTATION

There are few rules about presenting Indian food, but if you are entertaining have in mind which containers you will use for each dish and do not neglect the final decorative touches – the fresh coriander leaves, or the chopped chilli – that make the food look as appetising as it tastes. Curries and *dhaal* are served in large, deep dishes, rice is piled on flat oval dishes and *raita* (yogurt sauce) is best served in a bowl or sauce boat. Breads such as chapatis, paratas or pooris should be served on a plate wrapped in foil to keep them warm for as long as possible. Pickles, chutneys and *kachoomer* (onions and tomatoes in lemon juice) are eaten in small portions so it is best to put these in small bowls, each with a teaspoon in them, so that people do not take large helpings (in any case some of the pickles can be very hot and are certainly not intended to be eaten on their own).

Guests usually help themselves from the serving dishes. Rice is placed in the centre of the dinner plate, leaving some room for the curries, which are never put on top of the rice. It is not necessary to help yourself to everything on the table at once.

Though you will probably wish to provide a cruet set for the dinner table, it is a mistake for anyone to add salt before tasting, because it has always been added with all the other spices during cooking.

Decoration for the food, such as coriander leaves and green chillies, is best if fresh, but both of these items can be kept frozen in polythene bags or small freezer containers for convenience. Do not wash the coriander before freezing it: just rinse it under a cold tap before use. Coriander is fairly easy to grow in the back garden, especially during the summer months, and I have been reasonably successful growing it on the window-sill – so it is worth a try for this sometimes difficult-to-find herb. Other attractive and inexpensive garnishes include onion rings, tomatoes and lemon wedges.

By contrast, a rather special way of decorating both savoury dishes and desserts is to use *varq* (beaten silver leaf, which is edible). This method of decoration probably started with the Moghuls, perhaps seeking to intrigue their guests at palace banquets, and is reserved for special occasions because it is quite expensive. A dessert decorated with *varq* certainly looks beautiful, and is bound to impress your guests. It also provides quite a talking point. However, it is real silver, so it may not be very pleasant for anyone with fillings in their teeth.

As for cutlery, there is perhaps nothing better than traditional silver, which has been used in India for a long time, especially for more formal occasions. In family or less formal situations, however, it is still common for people to eat with the fingers of the right hand (considered the cleaner of the two), after both hands have been washed scrupulously.

Finally, if you want to clear your home of cooking smells after cooking Indian food, try lighting up a few incense sticks (*agar battis*) about an hour before the guests are due. I find these are far better than any air fresheners you can buy, and they come in various fragrances including jasmine and rose.

PLANNING MEALS

The dishes you choose to serve as a meal will depend upon the occasion. If you are having a supper party, for example, a *biryani* or *khichri* would make a very good centrepiece, and for a family meal you might prefer something less elaborate. The important thing to bear in mind is that protein in some form should be included, in the form of fish, *paneer*, or a pulse; lentil dishes, usually served as *dhaal*, are good complements for most vegetarian curries. I have indicated in each recipe whether the curry is 'wet', that is, with a sauce, or 'dry', and this should help you to combine textures for a varied spread.

Accompaniments such as chutneys and *kachoomers* are not a must, but I do feel they perk up a meal; *raitas* are also a nice complementary touch, to cool a hot curry or to freshen the palate. A typical vegetarian meal might consist of the following dishes: a vegetable curry, lentil dish, *kachoomer* or chutney, rice, and/or *aloo bondas* or *bhajias*, followed by dessert. Usually dishes are all served together, following no particular order as in other cuisines, but of course this is up to you.

VEGETABLES

The dishes in this section vary greatly in their taste, texture and in the degree to which they fill you up. Some may be eaten as a main dish (for example black-eyed bean and mushroom curry, on page 39), others are best served as part of a meal. I've made suggestions on how to serve and combine dishes to make a meal, but you will quickly learn to choose dishes that complement one another perfectly and, of course, you must follow your own tastebuds!

Aloo ki Tikki

POTATO ROUNDS

These delicious little potato rounds, coated with breadcrumbs and fried, are ideal served as teatime snacks or as part of a meal with a lentil dish.

Serves 4 (makes 10–12 tikkis)
2 large or 2 lb/900g potatoes
½ teaspoon ground coriander
1 teaspoon chilli powder
½ teaspoon *aamchoor* powder
1½ teaspoons salt
1 teaspoon chopped fresh mint
2 teaspoons chopped fresh coriander

1 small onion, peeled and finely chopped
1 egg, beaten
5 oz/140g fresh breadcrumbs
sufficient oil for shallow frying
mint leaves to garnish

Peel, boil and mash the potatoes and place in a large mixing bowl. Mix together all the spices, salt, mint, fresh coriander and onions, add to the potatoes and mix well. Break off small balls and flatten these in the palm of your hand. If the mixture is very sticky rub a little oil into your hands. Dip these rounds into the egg and then into the breadcrumbs, and set aside. Heat the oil in a frying pan and shallow-fry, turning once. Place on kitchen paper to remove excess oil.

Serve hot, garnished with fresh mint leaves.

Kajoo aur Aloo kay Kebab

CASHEW-NUT AND POTATO KEBABS

*S*erved *with a crisp green salad and sliced lemon, these 'kebabs'
make a delicious starter; served with a lentil dish and chapati they
are an excellent main meal. Use unsalted raw cashew-nuts.*

Serves 4

1 lb/450g potatoes, peeled and diced

4 oz/120g onion, peeled and diced

2 oz/60g peas

3 oz/90g cauliflower, cut into small florets

½ teaspoon diced and crushed ginger root

½ teaspoon crushed garlic

½ teaspoon chilli powder

1 teaspoon tomato purée

1 teaspoon salt

1 tablespoon chopped fresh coriander

2 oz/60g cashew-nuts, finely crushed

sufficient oil for shallow frying

Simmer the vegetables together until soft. Drain and leave in a sieve for about 5 minutes to remove excess moisture. Mash the vegetables and add the ginger, garlic, chilli, salt and tomato purée. Add the fresh coriander. Now mix in the cashew-nuts. Break off small balls of the vegetable mixture and pat them into flat circular shapes about ½ in/1cm thick with the palms of your hands. Heat the oil in a frying pan and fry gently over a medium heat, turning once.

Place on a kitchen towel to remove excess oil.

Aloo Methi

•••

POTATOES AND FENUGREEK

This aromatic curry originates in Hyderabad, where fenugreek grows abundantly and is widely used for cooking. A semi-dry curry, it is delicious served with Lemon Dhaal (page 47) and plain boiled rice. Whole red chillies are used in this; remember to discard these before serving as they can be fierce if you bite on them.

Serves 4
5 tablespoons corn oil
½ teaspoon onion seeds
2 medium onions
5 curry leaves
4 dried red chillies
1 tablespoon lemon juice
½ teaspoon diced and crushed
   ginger root
½ teaspoon crushed garlic
½ teaspoon chilli powder
1 bunch fresh fenugreek leaves
3 medium potatoes, peeled and
   diced
3 green chillies, halved
1 tablespoon chopped fresh
   coriander
¼ pint water

Heat the oil until quite hot and throw in the whole spices. After 30 seconds add the onions and fry in the oil until golden brown. Add the lemon juice, ginger, garlic, chilli powder and fenugreek leaves and stir-fry for about 2 minutes. Lower the heat and add the potatoes, green chillies and fresh coriander, and saute for a further minute to cook the potatoes with the spices. Pour in the water, cover and simmer for about 10 minutes, until the potatoes are tender.

Note Fresh fenugreek is widely used in Indian cooking, and these days is fairly easily obtainable all year round from Indian and Pakistani grocers. Use only the aromatic leaves, not the flowers which can taste bitter, and freeze them if you like in a carefully sealed plastic bag.

Aloo Bhindi

•••

CRISPY BITE-SIZE POTATOES AND OKRA

*T*he potatoes for this dish are fried to give them a delicious crisp coating. Always wash the okra before cutting as it becomes sticky once cut.

Serves 4

5 tablespoons corn oil

2 medium onions, peeled and sliced

3 dried red chillies

2 green chillies, deseeded and chopped if desired

2 tablespoons chopped fresh coriander

8 oz/225g okra, washed and cut into ½ in/1cm pieces

1 teaspoon salt

2 tablespoons lemon juice

3 tablespoons corn oil

1 teaspoon white cumin seeds

2 medium potatoes, peeled and roughly diced

1 tablespoon fresh coriander to garnish

Heat the corn oil until hot and fry the onions with the dried red chillies, green chillies and fresh coriander for 1 minute. Add the okra and salt and stir-fry for 5 minutes over a low heat. Sprinkle with lemon juice and set aside.

Heat the oil for the potatoes in a deep frying pan or *kadai* and fry the cumin seeds for a few minutes. Add the potatoes to the oil and fry until golden and cooked through. Remove from the heat and place on kitchen paper to remove excess oil.

Transfer the okra and the potatoes to a serving dish and serve garnished with fresh coriander.

Aloo ka Khorma

••

POTATOES KHORMA

These potatoes are cooked in a thick yogurty sauce and are very flavoursome. This curry makes a good dinner party dish, and is delicious served with paratha or chapati.

Serves 4

3 medium potatoes	½ teaspoon garam masala
1 large onion, peeled and sliced	¼ teaspoon black cumin seeds
5 tablespoons oil	3 green cardamoms
1 teaspoon salt	4 black peppercorns
1 teaspoon ginger root, diced and crushed	2 tablespoon natural yogurt
1 teaspoon crushed garlic	2 whole green chillies
1 teaspoon chilli powder	1 tablespoon fresh coriander
	¼ pt/150ml water

Peel and roughly dice the potatoes into about ½ in/1cm pieces. Place in a bowl of water to prevent discolouring and set aside. Fry the onions in hot oil until golden brown. Remove them with a slotted spoon, leaving the oil in the pan, and chop very finely or place in a food processor and process for about 30 seconds. Return the onions to the pan and add the salt and all the ground and whole spices (except the green chillies and fresh coriander) to the onions and fry for about a minute. Whip the yogurt and gradually add it to the onion mixture. Mix everything together and stir-fry for another minute, using a wooden spoon in semicircular movements. Add the potatoes, green chillies and fresh coriander. Stir well, and add the water. Simmer, covered, over a low heat for 5–7 minutes or until the potatoes are cooked through.

Garnish with more fresh coriander before serving.

Aloo aur Tamatar ka Khorma

••

POTATO AND TOMATO KHORMA

T his dish looks particularly attractive made with small whole new
potatoes and cherry tomatoes. It is a curry with a thick sauce, and
so would go well with a dry lentil dish, such as Spiced-up Moong
Dhaal, page 53, or Lemon Dhaal, page 47.

Serves 4

5 tablespoons natural yogurt	1 teaspoon desiccated coconut
1 teaspoon garam masala	3 cloves
1 teaspoon chilli powder	3 whole cardamoms
5 tablespoons corn oil	2 whole sticks of cinnamon
2 large onions, peeled and chopped	3 black peppercorns
1 teaspoon ginger root, diced and crushed	10 small whole new potatoes, scraped
1 teaspoon crushed garlic	¼ pint/150ml water
1½ teaspoons salt	8 cherry tomatoes
2 teaspoons ground almonds	2 tablespoons chopped fresh coriander
1 teaspoon poppy seeds	2 green chillies, deseeded and chopped if desired

Whip the yogurt in a bowl and mix in the garam masala and chilli
powder. Set aside.

Heat the oil and fry the onions until golden brown. Throw in all the
spices and seasonings and then add the yogurt mixture to the onions,
blending it in well. Stir-fry for about 2 minutes. Stir in the potatoes and
the water, cover and simmer for 5–7 minutes or until the potatoes are
cooked. Throw in the tomatoes, fresh coriander and green chillies.
Simmer for a further 2–3 minutes and serve immediately.

Note Green chillies give heat to curries. If you prefer a milder curry
discard the seeds, and reduce the quantity you use. I often add chopped
chillies at the end of cooking as this adds extra heat as well as colour. If
you like you can garnish curries with whole green chillies, for the very
brave, or you can serve a bowl on the side.

Saag Aloo

••

SPINACH AND POTATO CURRY

This semi-dry curry is a very popular dish, and is found on most Indian restaurant menus.

Serves 4
10 oz/300g fresh spinach or
   8 oz/225g frozen
1 large potato
5 tablespoons corn oil
¼ teaspoon onion seeds
¼ teaspoon mustard seeds
2 medium onions, peeled and
   chopped
1 tablespoon tomato purée
1 teaspoon crushed garlic

1 teaspoon diced and crushed
   ginger root
½ teaspoon ground coriander
½ teaspoon ground cumin
½ teaspoon chilli powder
¼ teaspoon turmeric
1 teaspoon salt
1 tablespoon lemon juice
1 tablespoon fresh coriander
¼ pint/150ml water

Wash the spinach thoroughly and chop finely. Add a little water and simmer until the spinach is soft. Drain well and set aside. Peel and dice the potato roughly and place in a bowl of water to prevent it discolouring. Heat the oil in a heavy-based saucepan, throw in the onion seeds and mustard seeds and fry these quickly until they darken a shade. Add the chopped onions and fry until golden brown.

Meanwhile place the tomato puree in a bowl and add all the remaining ingredients except the fresh coriander and water, and mix everything together. Pour this mixture over the onions and stir-fry for about 1½ minutes over a medium heat, scraping the bottom of the pan. Add the spinach and continue to stir-fry for at least 3–5 minutes or until it turns a shade darker. Add the potatoes and fresh coriander, lower the heat and add the water. Cover and simmer until the potatoes are cooked and the water has evaporated.

Serve hot with chapati or rice.

Note I can't detect a noticeable difference between fresh and frozen spinach in these recipes. I often use frozen simply because it spares me from the laborious and time-consuming task of washing the fresh leaves.

Sabut Baingun aur Aloo ka Salan

•••

WHOLE AUBERGINE AND POTATO CURRY

For this curry I use small whole aubergines, which are usually available from Indian or Pakistani grocers. If you have difficulty finding them, use ordinary aubergines cut into fairly large cubes.

Serves 4 as an accompaniment
5 tablespoons corn oil
2 medium onions, peeled and finely chopped
1 teaspoon crushed garlic
1 teaspoon ground ginger
4 green chillies, finely chopped
1 teaspoon ground cumin
5 small aubergines, whole, with stalks
2 tablespoons tomato purée
6 new potatoes, halved, with skins
1 teaspoon salt
1 medium onion, sliced
3 tablespoons chopped fresh coriander
¼ pint/150ml water

Heat the oil and fry the onions until golden brown. Add the garlic, ginger, green chillies and ground cumin. Add the aubergines and tomato purée and stir-fry for about 2 minutes. Now add the new potatoes, salt and sliced onion. Continue to stir-fry for a further 3 minutes. Add the fresh coriander and water, cover, lower the heat and simmer for about 10 minutes or until the potatoes and aubergines are tender.

Serve with a freshly made chapati and *kachoomer*.

Zeera Aloo

●●

POTATOES WITH CUMIN SEEDS

T his dry dish is eaten all over India. It is easy to cook and makes a delicious meal served with something as simple as a fried egg. Unless you can bear the heat, try not to bite on one of the whole chillies.

Serves 4
3 medium potatoes
5 tablespoons corn oil
½ teaspoon whole cumin seeds

3 curry leaves
3 dried red chillies
1 teaspoon salt

Wash, peel and slice the potatoes into ¼ in/5mm rounds. Place these in a bowl and cover with cold water to prevent discolouring.

In a deep frying pan heat the oil until hot and add the cumin seeds and curry leaves. Lower the heat to medium and add the dried red chillies. Fry until these turn a shade darker. Drain and pat dry the potatoes and add these to the seasoned oil. Add the salt and fry the potatoes until they are cooked through and some parts of the potatoes are darker than others.

Transfer to a serving dish and serve as an accompaniment to almost anything.

Masalay Walay Aloo

●●●

SPICED POTATOES

For this spicy potato dish I use mostly whole spices. Ideally you should use very small unpeeled whole new potatoes, easily available when in season. If you have difficulty finding these, just use roughly diced ordinary potatoes.

Serves 2–4
12 small new potatoes, unpeeled
2 teaspoons sesame seeds
4 tablespoons oil
4 spring onions (use whole of
  onion including green parts)
1 teaspoon salt
½ teaspoon white cumin seeds
½ teaspoon mustard seeds
4 curry leaves
2 green chillies, deseeded and slit
  down the middle
2 tablespoons fresh coriander

Wash and lightly boil the potatoes until just tender. Drain and set aside. Heat a heavy-based saucepan, add the sesame seeds and dry-roast them, covered, over a medium heat for about 2 minutes until golden brown, shaking the saucepan continuously to prevent them burning. Set aside. In the same pan heat the oil and fry the spring onions until soft, then add the salt and all the spices, including the green chillies and fresh coriander. Add the potatoes and stir-fry gently for about 3 minutes, taking care not to break the potatoes. Finally, throw in the sesame seeds and shake the pan so that the potatoes are well coated.

Serve hot.

Haray Masalay ki Subzee

SPICED VEGETABLES FRIED IN GREEN HERBS

*T*his fairly dry dish is best served with a wet lentil dish and plain boiled rice.

Serves 4
2 bunches spring onions
4 tablespoons corn oil
1 bunch fresh coriander, chopped
4 fresh or dried curry leaves
10 new potatoes, scraped and halved
6 oz/175g cut green beans

3 fresh green chillies, cut into ½ in/1cm pieces, deseeded if desired
1 teaspoon salt
¼ pint/150ml water
3 fresh green chillies to garnish, deseeded and chopped if desired

Prepare the spring onions by washing, topping and tailing them, and cutting them up, green and white parts, into 1 in/2.5cm pieces. Heat the oil and fry them lightly until just soft, then throw in the fresh coriander, reserving a handful for garnish, and the curry leaves. Stir around over a medium heat with a wooden spoon. Now add the potatoes and cut green beans. Continue to stir-fry, add the cut green chillies and stir in the salt. Add the water, lower the heat, cover and simmer for 10–15 minutes or until the potatoes are cooked through.

Garnish with the fresh green chillies, chopped and deseeded or whole, as desired, and the remaining fresh coriander.

Notes When chopping green chillies always remember to wash your hands afterwards with soap, and never touch any part of the face as it can sting very badly.

Fresh curry leaves are available from Indian and Pakistani grocers. Though it is best to use fresh leaves, dried ones may be substituted.

Sarson ka Saag

••

BUTTERY MUSTARD LEAVES

This curry is a great favourite in the Punjab. Similar in appearance and flavour to ordinary spinach, mustard leaves are cooked here in butter or ghee, with a few spices. They are best served with chapati.

Serves 4
12 oz/340g mustard leaves, fresh
  or canned
1 teaspoon corn oil
4 oz/120g ghee or butter

½ teaspoon white cumin seeds
½ teaspoon crushed garlic
½ teaspoon chilli powder
1 teaspoon salt

Cook the fresh mustard leaves in a little water until soft, then drain. (If you are using canned mustard leaves, simply drain any excess water.) Set aside.

Heat the oil and butter together, add the white cumin seeds and fry until they darken a shade. Add the remaining spices and salt and finally the mustard leaves, fry for about 3–5 minutes until it turns darker, stirring continuously. Turn off the heat and let it stand for about 2 minutes.

Serve hot.

Notes Ghee – clarified fat – is made either from pure butter, in which case it is called *usli ghee*, or 'real ghee', or, more commonly, from a mixture of vegetable oils. It is readily available from all Indian grocers, or you can make it as described on pages 134–5.

Mustard leaves are found in Indian and Pakistani grocers. If you like you can substitute spinach for the mustard leaves, and this is just as good.

Tamatar Methi

●●

TOMATOES AND FRESH FENUGREEK

I prefer to use canned tomatoes for this curry as they give a richer texture and a thicker sauce. Decorate this dish with hard-boiled eggs and serve with the rice recipe on page 72.

Serves 4
1 teaspoon diced and crushed
  ginger root
1 teaspoon crushed garlic
¼ teaspoon turmeric
1 teaspoon chilli powder
1 teaspoon salt
2 teaspoons lemon juice
14 oz/400g canned tomatoes
4 tablespoons oil

2 medium onions, peeled and
  chopped
3 oz/90g fresh fenugreek leaves
  (see note on page 12)
2 green chillies, chopped and
  deseeded if desired
3 hard-boiled eggs, halved
1 tablespoon fresh coriander

Combine all the spices, salt and lemon juice with the canned tomatoes, mix well and set aside. Heat the oil and fry the onions until golden brown. Add the fresh fenugreek leaves and stir-fry for about 2 minutes over a low heat. Add the tomato mixture and stir in a semicircular movement for 3–5 minutes or until the sauce has thickened. Throw in the green chillies.

Transfer to a serving bowl and decorate with the hard-boiled eggs and fresh coriander.

Gobi ki Bhujia

•••

CAULIFLOWER BHUJIA

T his is a dry curry and is particularly aromatic because of the whole
spices used, especially the curry leaves. It is delicious served with a
freshly made paratha (page 115).

Serves 4

4 tablespoons corn oil
½ teaspoon onion seeds
½ teaspoon mustard seeds
½ teaspoon white cumin seeds
4 curry leaves
1 large onion, peeled and sliced
2 cloves garlic
4 dried red chillies
1 teaspoon salt
2 green chillies, chopped
8 oz/225g cauliflower, cut into
  small florets
2 tablespoons chopped fresh
  coriander

Heat the oil in a heavy-based saucepan and fry all the whole seeds and
curry leaves until a shade darker. Add the onion, garlic, dried red
chillies and salt. Fry until the onions almost begin to caramelise but
not burn (remove from the heat at this stage if necessary). Add the
whole green chillies, cauliflower and coriander and stir-fry until tender
and some parts of the cauliflower are darker than others.

Serve immediately.

Pyaaz Bharay Karelay

••

STUFFED BITTER GOURD

Unless you are familiar with cooking bitter gourds (or karela, *as they are sometimes known*), you will be surprised at how bitter they can be. You can get rid of some of this bitterness by discarding the seeds, and salting and leaving the flesh for 2 hours to let the salt draw out the bitter juices. However, the sharpness does make a good contrast flavour to your table, and I find this crispy stuffed karela quite delicious. Do try it – you may well acquire a taste for it.

Serves 4

6 bitter gourds (about 1½–2 lb/675–900g)
2 tablespoons salt
2 oz/60g *chana dhaal* (yellow split peas)
3 tablespoons corn oil
2 medium onions, peeled and chopped
¼ teaspoon fenugreek seeds
1 teaspoon ground coriander
1 teaspoon crushed garlic

1 teaspoon chilli powder
½ teaspoon salt
1 tablespoon lemon juice
2 tablespoons chopped fresh coriander

BAGHAAR (SEASONED OIL)
4 tablespoons oil
3 curry leaves
½ teaspoon onion seeds

3 green chillies to garnish

Wash the bitter gourds and cut in half lengthwise; remove and discard the seeds. Place the gourds on a plate, flesh side up, and sprinkle with the salt. Set aside. Boil the *chana dhaal* in 1 pint/600ml water for about 20–25 minutes until soft but not mushy. Drain and set aside. Meanwhile, heat the oil in a saucepan and fry the onions until golden brown. Lower the heat and add the fenugreek seeds, ground coriander, garlic, chilli powder, salt, lemon juice and fresh coriander. Stir-fry these well together for 2–3 minutes. Stir in the *chana dhaal* and set this mixture aside. Rinse the bitter gourds thoroughly to get rid of the salt, pat dry and stuff each one with the onion mixture.

To make the *baghaar*, heat the oil in a frying pan and fry the curry leaves and onion seeds. Fry the bitter gourds gently on all sides in the *baghaar* for 2–3 minutes, or until they turn a shade darker. Remove carefully from the pan and place on an oval serving dish. Garnish with fresh whole green chillies.

Phalli/Tamatar aur Kairi

•••

GREEN BEANS AND MANGO

*R*aw mango, or kairi *as it is known in Urdu, is used more commonly in pickles and chutneys, but when used in curries it adds a lovely tangy flavour. This curry is simple to cook and is delicious mopped up with chapati. Try to use the beans available at Indian or Pakistani grocers if you can; otherwise any green beans will do.*

Serves 4
8 oz/225g whole green beans cut
   into ½ in/1cm pieces
½ teaspoon mustard seeds
½ teaspoon onion seeds
4 curry leaves
4 whole dried red chillies

2 tablespoons chopped fresh
   coriander
1 teaspoon salt
3 tomatoes, diced
1 small unripe mango, diced
2 green chillies, finely chopped

Simmer the green beans until just tender and set aside. Heat the oil until very hot, remove from the heat and drop in the whole spices. Over the heat, add the fresh coriander, salt and tomatoes and stir-fry for about 2 minutes. Now add the diced mango and the green beans and stir-fry for about 5–7 minutes. Garnish with chopped green chillies.

Note It is essential to buy *unripe* mango for this dish, for its sour, sharp flavour; you will usually find them in stock at Indian and Pakistani grocers.

Shalgam ka Salan

•••

BABY TURNIP CURRY

I do not cook turnips very often, but when I do I usually choose this particular way of cooking them, which is deliciously tangy and especially good when served with a freshly made chapati and a pickle.

Serves 4
3 baby turnips or 1 lb/450g large
  turnip
4 tablespoons oil
2 medium onions, peeled and
  finely chopped
1 teaspoon salt
½ teaspoon chilli powder
½ teaspoon garam masala

½ teaspoon diced and crushed
  ginger root
a pinch turmeric
4 tablespoons natural yogurt
2 tablespoons chopped fresh
  coriander
3 green chillies, finely chopped
½ pint/300ml water

Wash, peel and roughly chop up the turnips. Cover with cold water to prevent discoloration. Heat the oil in a deep pan and fry the onions until golden brown. Lower the heat and add the salt and spices, whip the yogurt lightly with a fork and add to the onion mixture. Stir-fry for about 2 minutes, then mix in the drained turnips, fresh coriander and green chillies. Add the water, and simmer, covered, over a low heat until the turnips are cooked.

Serve hot.

Bhindi Dopiaza

•••

OKRA DOPIAZA

The word dopiaza *means, literally, 'two onion', or 'double onion', and an Indian dish with 'dopiaza' in its name simply means that onions are a major ingredient. In this dish they are combined with okra or* bhindi *(also known as lady's fingers).* Bhindi *should always be washed before you cut them as they become sticky once cut.*

Serves 4
5 tablespoons corn oil
1 lb/450g onions, peeled and
    sliced
½ teaspoon onion seeds
4 curry leaves
4 dried red chillies
1 medium tomato, sliced
½ teaspoon ginger root, diced
    and crushed

½ teaspoon chilli powder
½ teaspoon crushed garlic
1 teaspoon salt
8 oz/225g okra, washed and cut
    into 1 in/2.5cm pieces
2 tablespoons chopped fresh
    coriander
2 green chillies (finely chopped
    and deseeded if desired)

Heat the oil in a large, deep frying pan and fry the onions along with the onion seeds, curry leaves and dried red chillies. When the onions are golden brown add the sliced tomato, the ginger root, chilli powder, garlic and salt. Turn the heat to low and throw in the okra pieces. Stir-fry for 5–7 minutes, taking care not to mash them up as they soften.

Sprinkle with the fresh coriander and green chillies, and serve hot with chapati.

Baingun aur Pyaaz ki Bhujia

•••

AUBERGINE AND ONION CURRY

For this dry vegetable curry, it is best to chop both the onion and aubergine finely so that the aubergine cooks fairly quickly and gives the maximum flavour. This dish is best served with the lentil curry on page 46 and chapati.

Serves 4

2 medium onions, peeled and finely chopped

8 oz/225g aubergine, finely chopped

4 tablespoons chopped fresh coriander

4 tablespoons oil

3 curry leaves, fresh or dried

½ teaspoon onion/mustard/fenugreek seeds

1 teaspoon salt

1 tablespoon lemon juice

Prepare the onions and aubergines and mix 1 tablespoon of the fresh coriander with each. Heat the oil with the curry leaves and the whole spices. When the oil is hot add the finely chopped onions, and fry until soft and golden brown. Add the remaining fresh coriander, salt and the finely chopped aubergines. Lower the heat and fry gently and patiently for at least 15 minutes or until the aubergines are tender. Check by pressing down with a wooden spoon. Sprinkle in the lemon juice, lower the heat and simmer for 3–5 minutes.

Mayvay ka Salan

••

FRUITY CURRY

Fruit *is hardly ever used in authentic traditional curries; this is a typical anglicised version of a curry, using apples and sultanas. It is good served with plain boiled rice.*

Serves 4
1 lb/450g cooking apples
few drops of lemon juice
12 oz/340g onion, peeled and
  chopped
4 tablespoons corn oil
½ teaspoon ground cumin
½ teaspoon ground coriander
2 whole bay leaves

1 lb/450g mushrooms, wiped or
  peeled and sliced
3 oz/90g sultanas
1 teaspoon salt
1 teaspoon freshly ground black
  pepper
4 tablespoons fresh single cream
1 tablespoon fresh coriander

Peel and dice the apples and place in a bowl of water with a few drops of lemon juice to prevent them discolouring.

Fry the chopped onions in the oil until golden brown. Lower the heat and add the cumin, coriander and bay leaves. Stir-fry for a further minute. Add the mushrooms and sultanas, and continue to stir-fry while gradually adding the remaining ingredients, finally adding the cream and fresh coriander. Cover and simmer for 2 minutes before serving.

Mirch ka Salan

••

SPICY STUFFED GREEN PEPPER CURRY

This typically *Hyderabadi curry is traditionally made with large green chillies, and every Hyderabadi is expected to know how to cook it. Highly spiced and almost like a pickle, it is served as a side dish decorated with hard-boiled eggs, and is ideal for a dinner party. The recipe given here uses large green peppers instead of green chillies, so that it is not unbearably hot. Three large peppers are generally enough as a side dish for four people.*

Serves 4

3 green peppers
2 tablespoons desiccated coconut
1 tablespoon sesame seeds
6 tablespoons corn oil
4 medium onions, peeled and
   finely chopped
1½ teaspoons ground cumin
1½ teaspoons ground coriander
1 teaspoon diced and crushed
   ginger root
1 teaspoon crushed garlic
1½ teaspoons chilli powder
¼ teaspoon turmeric
1 teaspoon salt
1 tablespoon tamarind paste (see
   Note)

¼ pint/150ml water
2 tablespoons chopped fresh
   coriander

BAGHAAR (SEASONED OIL)
4 tablespoons corn oil
¼ teaspoon white cumin seeds
¼ teaspoon onion seeds
¼ teaspoon mustard seeds
¼ teaspoon fenugreek seeds
4 curry leaves
3 dried red chillies

3 hard-boiled eggs, halved, to
   garnish

Wash and cut the tops off the green peppers, remove the seeds, pat dry and set aside. Dry-roast the coconut and sesame seeds by placing them in a saucepan over a hot stove. Cover the pan and shake it continuously over the heat for about 2 minutes. Remove from the heat and grind in a coffee grinder or food processor. Heat the oil and fry the onions until golden brown. Add the ground coconut and sesame seeds, the cumin, coriander, ginger, garlic, chilli powder, turmeric and salt. Lower the heat and cook, stirring continuously for 2–3 minutes. Remove from the heat and leave to cool. Stuff the peppers with this onion and spice mixture.

To make the *baghaar*, heat the oil and fry the whole seeds, curry leaves and dried red chillies for about a minute, until they turn a shade darker. Lower the heat and add the stuffed peppers, moving them around gently with a wooden spoon. Fry for 2 minutes. Mix the tamarind paste with the water until smooth, and pour over the peppers. Add the fresh coriander, cover and simmer for about 10–15 minutes, stirring occasionally. Arrange on a serving dish and garnish with the hard-boiled eggs.

Note You can either make your own tamarind paste from the dried fruit (obtainable from Indian grocers) or, more simply, buy the ready-made gooey brown paste in jars. Once opened, this paste will keep for 2–3 months.

Patta Gobi aur Pyaaz ki Bhujia

●●●

SPICY WHITE CABBAGE AND ONION CURRY

A very dry curry mostly eaten in the south of India, this dish includes curry leaves and onion seeds which make it not only attractive but also very aromatic. Serve hot with chapati and a lime pickle.

Serves 4
4 tablespoons corn oil
1 level teaspoon onion seeds
3 curry leaves
3 dried red chillies
2 medium onions, peeled and
    sliced
1 teaspoon salt

½ teaspoon chilli powder
2 cloves garlic
6 oz/175g white cabbage,
    chopped
1 tablespoon lemon juice
1 tablespoon fresh coriander,
    chopped
¼ pint/150ml water

Heat the oil in a saucepan. Throw in the onion seeds, curry leaves and whole red chillies. Lower the heat, add the onions and fry until golden brown. Add the salt and remaining spices and stir-fry for about a minute. Now add the white cabbage, lemon juice and fresh coriander and continue to stir-fry for about 2 minutes. Increase the heat, add the water and bring to the boil, cover and simmer for 5–7 minutes or until the water is absorbed and the cabbage is cooked.

Makhani Saag

••

BUTTERED SPINACH

This recipe is a favourite of mine, especially when I use fresh spinach (frozen may be substituted). Served with freshly made chapati it is delicious.

Serves 4
12 oz/340g fresh spinach
3 oz butter
1 tablespoon corn oil
2 onions, peeled and chopped
2 cloves

2 cinnamon sticks
1 teaspoon salt
3 cloves garlic
½ teaspoon ginger root, shredded
1 teaspoon chilli powder
2 green chillies to garnish

Wash and chop the spinach finely and simmer for about 15 minutes. Drain all the water and squeeze or press down in a strainer to remove excess water. Heat the butter and oil together and fry the onion until soft. Then add all the remaining ingredients except the green chillies. Lower the heat and stir-fry the mixture for about 20 seconds. Mix in the spinach and continue to stir-fry in semicircular movements for about 10 minutes, or until the spinach darkens. Add the green chillies, either chopped or whole, and serve.

Thali Huwi Subzee (1)

●●●

CRUNCHY FRIED VEGETABLES

T*he majority of Indian vegetables are cooked until they are soft, but this is one recipe in which they remain crunchy. Best eaten as soon as it is ready, this dish should be served as part of a meal.*

Serves 4
4 tablespoons corn oil
½ teaspoon mustard seeds
4 curry leaves
½ teaspoon onion seeds
6 dried red chillies
3 courgettes, cut into ¼ in/6mm
   slices
4 carrots, cut thinly into 1 in/
   2.5cm long pieces

4 oz/120g green beans, cut into
   1 in/2.5cm pieces
8 baby corns
6 oz/180g cauliflower
1 teaspoon salt
2 tablespoons desiccated coconut

GARNISH
mint leaves
2 limes

Heat the oil in a large deep saucepan and throw in the whole spices. Gradually add all the vegetables and sprinkle with the salt. Sauté the vegetables for about 7 minutes, stirring gently with a slotted steel spoon to prevent them being broken up. Sprinkle over the desiccated coconut and stir it in well.

Serve immediately, garnished with mint leaves and lime wedges.

Thali Huwi Subzee (2)

••

SPICY SAUTÉED VEGETABLES

This delicious spicy mixture of vegetables is quick and easy to prepare, and will go well with almost anything.

Serves 4
3 oz/90g sweet corn kernels
3 oz/90g mushrooms, roughly sliced
2 oz/60g red peppers, roughly sliced
3 oz/90g cauliflower florets
3 oz/90g fresh or frozen peas

4 tablespoons corn oil
½ teaspoon onion seeds
2 cloves garlic, crushed
½ teaspoon crushed dried red chillies
1 teaspoon salt
3 fresh mint leaves
2 mint leaves to garnish

Wash and prepare all the vegetables, mix them together and leave covered in a bowl. Over a high heat, heat the oil in a deep non-stick frying pan and throw in the onion seeds, wait until they turn a shade darker and then add the garlic. Lower the heat to medium, add the mixed vegetables and stir-fry for about 3 minutes. Add the crushed red chillies and salt and cook for a further minute. Finally add the mint leaves and mix well.

Garnish with mint leaves and serve hot.

Podinay ki Subzee

MINTY MIXED VEGETABLES

*T*his colourful mixture of vegetables is sautéed lightly in a blend of yogurt, mint and spicy onions.

Serves 4

2 medium carrots, peeled and sliced

2 medium potatoes, peeled and roughly diced

4 oz/120g sliced green beans

4 tablespoons corn oil

2 medium onions, peeled and chopped

1 teaspoon chilli powder

1 teaspoon ground coriander

1 teaspoon crushed garlic

1 teaspoon salt

4 teaspoons natural yogurt

2 tablespoons chopped fresh mint leaves

1 tablespoon chopped fresh coriander

3–4 mint leaves to garnish

Simmer the carrots, potatoes and beans in salted water until just tender but not mushy. Drain and set aside. Heat the oil in a deep frying pan and fry the onions until golden brown. Meanwhile mix together the ground spices, garlic and salt with the yogurt. Pour this over the onions and stir-fry for about 2 minutes, scraping the bottom of the pan. When the mixture begins to darken and thicken a little, add the vegetables and sauté for about 3 minutes, stirring gently so that you do not mash the potatoes. Sprinkle in the fresh mint and coriander and mix in.

Serve garnished with mint leaves.

Dam ki Subzee

••

BAKED VEGETABLES WITH WHOLE SPICES AND CHEESE

This dish is rather unusual because Indian dishes are almost always cooked on top of the stove, rarely in the oven. It is also unusual in that it includes Cheddar cheese, which is seldom used in the Indian kitchen. The vegetables, lightly sautéed and then baked with a topping of Cheddar cheese and tomatoes, are delicious served with a green salad.

Serves 4

3 oz/90g butter plus 1 tablespoon corn oil
¼ teaspoon black cumin seeds
2 cinnamon sticks
1 medium onion, peeled and finely chopped
6 oz/180g cauliflower, cut into small florets
4 oz/120g potatoes, cut into thin chips

4 oz/120g green beans, fresh or frozen
1 teaspoon salt
1 teaspoon coarsely ground black pepper
1 tablespoon lemon juice
8 oz/225g Cheddar cheese, grated
2 medium tomatoes, sliced
1 tablespoon chopped fresh coriander

Heat the butter and oil in a deep frying pan, throw in the whole spices and onion, and stir-fry until golden brown. One by one add all the other vegetables, the seasoning and lemon juice. Continue to fry for 3–5 minutes over a medium heat. Remove from the heat and put the vegetables in an ovenproof dish, spread the grated cheese evenly on top and place the sliced tomatoes over the cheese. Sprinkle the chopped fresh coriander over the top and bake in a preheated oven (400°F/200°C/Gas 6) for 12–15 minutes.

Serve hot.

Miloni Subzee

••

MIXED VEGETABLE CURRY

*T*his hot and spicy vegetable curry is delicious with plain boiled rice and any chutney. A mixed vegetable curry like this is a good way of using up leftover vegetables from the fridge.

Serves 4

4 tablespoons corn oil

1 teaspoon mixed onion, mustard and white cumin seeds

2 medium onions, peeled and chopped

1 teaspoon chilli powder

1 teaspoon diced and crushed ginger root

½ teaspoon ground coriander

½ teaspoon ground cumin

1 teaspoon crushed garlic

1 teaspoon salt

2 tablespoons tomato purée

1 tablespoon lemon juice

2 fresh tomatoes, diced

3 oz/90g cauliflower, cut into small florets

3 oz/90g diced aubergine

4 oz/120g fresh green beans, cut into ½ in/1cm pieces

2 tablespoons chopped fresh coriander

¼ pint/150ml water

Heat the oil in a heavy-based saucepan until quite hot, add all the seeds and wait until they turn a shade darker before adding the onions and frying these until golden brown. Lower the heat and gradually add the spices, garlic, salt, tomato purée and lemon juice, and stir-fry for about 2 minutes. Add the diced tomatoes and all the other vegetables and mix well to coat the vegetables with the spices. Add the fresh coriander and water, cover and simmer until the vegetables are tender. Remove the lid and stir occasionally until the oil separates.

Serve hot with poori.

Mili Huwi Subzee

••

MIXED VEGETABLES IN A CREAMY TOMATO SAUCE

You may add any other vegetable of your choice to this creamy curry. You could use yogurt instead of the cream, for a slightly sharper flavour.

Serves 4

6 tablespoons corn oil

½ teaspoon mixed onion and mustard seeds

3 curry leaves

14 oz/400g can chopped tomatoes

1 teaspoon diced and crushed ginger root

½ teaspoon chilli powder

1 teaspoon ground coriander

½ teaspoon ground cumin

1 teaspoon crushed garlic

1 teaspoon salt

2 tablespoons chopped fresh coriander

3 oz/90g potatoes, peeled and diced

3 oz/90g cauliflower florets

3 tablespoons fresh single cream

Heat the oil in a heavy saucepan. Add the onion and mustard seeds along with the curry leaves, and lower the heat a little. Add the chopped tomatoes, spices, garlic, salt and fresh coriander. Stir-fry for 2–3 minutes. Now add the potatoes and cauliflower and continue to stir-fry for a further 2 minutes. Lower the heat further, cover and simmer until the potatoes are cooked, adding a little water if required.

Stir in the fresh cream and serve hot.

Lobia aur Kumbi ka Salan

•••

BLACK-EYED BEAN AND MUSHROOM CURRY

Mushrooms are not eaten widely in India, but when I came to England I just loved them, fried, in an omelette or cooked using a few spices. This recipe is easy to prepare, and is delicious served hot with poori or paratha and kachoomer (page 104).

Serves 4
4 oz/120g black-eyed beans
10 oz /280g mushrooms
4 tablespoons corn oil
2 medium onions, peeled and
  sliced
½ teaspoon diced and crushed
  ginger root

½ teaspoon crushed garlic
½ teaspoon chilli powder
¼ teaspoon turmeric
1 teaspoon salt
2 tomatoes, cut into wedges
2 tablespoons chopped fresh
  coriander

Boil the black-eyed beans until soft (about half an hour) and set aside. Peel or wipe the mushrooms and slice them thinly. Using a deep non-stick frying pan, heat the oil and fry the onions until golden brown. Lower the heat and add the spices, including the salt. Stir for about 30 seconds. Add the mushrooms and sauté for about 3–5 minutes before adding the tomato wedges, black-eyed beans and fresh coriander. Stir for a further 3–5 minutes and serve.

Lobia aur Saag

●●●

BLACK-EYED BEANS WITH SPINACH

T*his nourishing dish is tastier if made with fresh spinach, although frozen may be used. It makes an attractive party dish. Serve with the rice dish on page 83.*

Serves 4 (as part of a meal)
12 oz/340g fresh spinach
4 oz/120g black-eyed beans
2 medium onions, peeled and
   chopped
5 tablespoons corn oil
½ teaspoon ground cumin

½ teaspoon ground coriander
1 teaspoon chilli powder
1 teaspoon crushed garlic
1 teaspoon salt
1 tablespoon tomato purée
2 tablespoons chopped fresh
   coriander

Wash the spinach thoroughly, chop very finely and simmer in a little lightly salted water until soft. Drain well, place in a bowl and set aside. Boil the black-eyed beans until soft (about half an hour) and set aside.

Meanwhile, fry the onions in the oil in a heavy-based saucepan. Combine the spices, garlic and salt with the tomato purée to make a thick paste. Pour this paste over the onions and stir-fry for about a minute. Now add the spinach and fresh coriander, and stir-fry for about 5 minutes until most of the liquid has evaporated and the spinach is darker in colour. Add the black-eyed beans, mix well, lower the heat, cover and cook for 2–4 minutes.

Serve hot.

Kabli Chana

••

CHICK PEA CURRY

I *always keep a few cans of chick peas in my larder as they are very useful for making a quick curry. If you use dried chick peas it is best to soak them overnight before boiling them until soft. This is quite a filling dish, best served with light vegetables or a raita, and hot poori (see page 117).*

Serves 4
5 tablespoons corn oil
3 curry leaves
2 medium onions, peeled and chopped
¼ teaspoon fenugreek seeds
1 teaspoon diced and crushed ginger root
1 teaspoon ground coriander
½ teaspoon chilli powder
1 teaspoon crushed garlic
1 teaspoon salt

2 tablespoons tomato purée
3 tablespoons chopped fresh coriander
2 medium tomatoes, sliced
16 oz/450g can chick peas, *or* 10 oz/280g dried chick peas
1 large potato, peeled and diced
2 green chillies, chopped, deseeded if desired
¼ pint/150ml water
fresh coriander to garnish

Heat the oil in a saucepan, add the curry leaves and onions, stir and fry until the onions are soft and golden. In a small bowl mix together all the spices, garlic and salt along with the tomato purée. Blend this paste well with the onions, lower the heat and simmer for about a minute. Next add the fresh coriander, tomatoes, chick peas, potato, green chillies and the water and mix well. Cover the saucepan, lower the heat and simmer until the potatoes are tender.

Serve hot, garnished with fresh coriander.

Spicy Vegetable Pancakes

••

*T*his impressive dish is an unusual Indian creation. If you make the pancakes smaller they would make a delightful starter.

Serves 4

FILLING
3 medium potatoes, peeled and sliced
3 oz/90g peas
2 oz/60g sweetcorn
3 oz/90g carrots, peeled and sliced
1 tablespoon tomato purée
2 tablespoons corn oil
½ teaspoon onion seeds
½ teaspoon chilli powder
½ teaspoon crushed garlic
1 teaspoon salt
2 oz/60g chopped fresh coriander

BATTER
6 oz/80g plain flour
2 eggs
½ pint/300ml milk
3 oz/90g butter

GARNISH
1 small onion, peeled and chopped
2 medium tomatoes, diced
1 oz/30g fresh coriander, chopped
2 green chillies, chopped
1 lemon, cut in wedges

To make the filling, simmer all the vegetables together until they are soft enough to be mashed. Drain, mash and then blend with the tomato purée. Set aside. Heat the oil in a deep frying pan and add the onion seeds. When they begin to splutter put the vegetable mixture into the oil and stir-fry. Add the chilli powder, garlic, salt and fresh coriander. Remove from the pan, place in a bowl and leave to cool.

To make the pancake batter, sieve the flour, beat the eggs and mix into the flour gradually, along with the milk. Whip to break up any balls of flour and make into a smooth batter. (This can be done in a food processor.) Heat the pancake pan and melt in it about ½ teaspoon of butter. With a deep spoon pour in enough batter to cover the bottom of the pan, tilting the pan in order to spread the mixture evenly and fairly thinly. When bubbles begin to form, turn over the pancake. Remove when golden and cooked, and keep warm. This will make 6–8 pancakes, depending on the size of the pancake pan.

To serve, place two pancakes on each plate and spoon the vegetable mixture evenly into each pancake. Roll up the pancakes and garnish with the chopped onion, diced tomato, fresh coriander, chopped green chilli and lemon wedges.

Masala aur Subzee ka Omelette

SPICY VEGETARIAN OMELETTE

*E*ggs *are usually eaten at breakfast time in India, fried, boiled or made into a delicious spicy omelette such as this one. It is a very good way of using up leftovers.*

Serves 2–3
1 medium potato
3 tablespoons corn oil
1 medium onion, peeled and
   sliced
1 clove garlic, crushed
½ teaspoon salt
1 teaspoon chilli powder

2 green chillies, chopped,
   deseeded if desired
2 tablespoons chopped fresh
   coriander
6 button mushrooms, halved
1 medium tomato, chopped
4 medium eggs

Peel, boil and mash the potato, add a little salt to taste and set aside. Heat the oil in a thick deep frying pan and fry the onion until soft golden brown. Lower the heat, add the garlic, salt, chilli powder, green chillies, fresh coriander, mushrooms and tomato and fry everything together. Gradually add the mashed potato.

Beat the four eggs lightly and pour over the vegetable mixture. Let the eggs cook slowly for about 1½ minutes. Turn the mixture very gently and cook the other side for a further minute.

This is delicious served with a *kachoomer* and mango chutney.

Karahi Paneer

•••

KARAHI CHEESE

Paneer, *a delicate white cheese resembling cottage cheese in flavour, is eaten widely in India, especially by vegetarians, as a source of protein. In this rather unusual way of cooking it, the cheese is sautéed in a* karahi *with onions, small whole tomatoes and spices. It is delicious eaten with poori.*

Serves 4
4 tablespoons corn oil
1 large onion, peeled and
  chopped
1 teaspoon diced and crushed
  ginger root
1 teaspoon chilli powder
1 teaspoon salt

2 firm tomatoes, cut into quarters
2 green chillies, chopped and
  deseeded if desired
2 tablespoons chopped fresh
  coriander
10–12 1 in/2.5cm cubes of
  paneer (see below)

Fry the onions in a sauté pan, or a *karahi* if you have one, until a soft golden brown. Lower the heat and gradually add all the spices. Add the tomatoes, green chillies and half the fresh coriander. Now add the cubed cheese and stir-fry for about 2–3 minutes. Serve garnished with the remaining fresh coriander.

Paneer

Simmer 1¾ pints/1 litre of full cream milk over a low heat, then add 2 tablespoons lemon juice, stirring continuously and gently for about an hour or more until the milk thickens and begins to curdle. Strain the curdled milk through a sieve. Put the curds in a bowl and place under a heavy weight for about 1½–2 hours to press to a flat shape about ½ in/1cm thick. Once set, the *paneer* can be cut, like cheese, into cubes. It will keep for about 24 hours in the refrigerator.

LENTILS
AND PULSES

L entils (dhaals) *provide a vital source of protein for the vegetarian, and in Indian cooking as many as thirty different varieties are used. They are most commonly served as accompaniments, but are also cooked with meat and vegetables.*

In India regional differences affect which dhaals are favoured, and of course personal preference. My mother swears by masoor *and uses no other; my sister-in-law cooks with only two, and I enjoy six or seven types. The four I use most frequently, however, are:* masoor, *the common red lentil found easily in supermarkets;* chana, *dark yellow, pea-size split lentils;* urid, *tiny white split lentils, quite dry when cooked; and* moong, *small yellow split lentils.* Toor dhaal, *another favourite of mine, resembles the split pea, though it is darker in colour and oilier.*

It is wise to pick over lentils before cooking to remove any stones or husks and to wash them thoroughly. If you choose to cook a dry curry, always serve a wet dhaal *with it and vice versa.*

All of these lentils are stocked by Indian and Pakistani grocers where they are packaged with their Indian rather than their English names. It is worth seeking them out, as each is quite different in appearance, texture and flavour, and you will come to have your own favourites.

Saadhi Dhaal

SIMPLE DHAAL

This basic dhaal *is easy to cook and ideal served with rice and any other vegetable curry.*

Serves 4

4 oz/120g *masoor dhaal*
4 oz/120g *chana dhaal*
1 teaspoon diced and crushed
  ginger root
1 teaspoon crushed garlic
½ teaspoon turmeric
1 tablespoon chopped fresh
  coriander
1½ pints/1350ml water
1½ teaspoons salt

BAGHAAR (SEASONED OIL)

1 tablespoon butter and a little
  oil
1 medium onion, peeled and
  sliced
½ tablespoon mixed mustard
  and onion seeds
3 whole fresh *or* dried curry
  leaves

Pick over and wash the lentils. Place all the *dhaal* ingredients, except the salt, in a saucepan with 1 pint/600ml water and cook over a medium heat for 15–20 minutes or until the water has evaporated and the lentils are soft enough to be mashed into a paste-like consistency. Add the salt and ½ pint/300ml water, return to the heat and bring to the boil. Turn off the heat.

To make the *baghaar*, heat the butter and oil together, add the onion, mustard and onion seeds and curry leaves, and fry until golden brown. Pour over the lentils and serve.

Khatti Dhaal

●●

LEMON DHAAL

*T*his typical Hyderabadi lentil dish was cooked almost every day in
our house as a side dish. I also remember that my nanny, who was
a wet nurse to my mother, cooked it the best. A versatile dhaal, *it can
be served as a side dish with almost anything. The addition of* baghaar
before serving gives it an extra spicy lift.

Serves 4 as a side dish
6 oz/180g *masoor dhaal*
1½ pints/900ml water
1 teaspoon chilli powder
4 curry leaves
½ teaspoon diced and crushed
   ginger root
½ teaspoon crushed garlic
¼ teaspoon turmeric
1 teaspoon salt
2 tomatoes, cut into quarters

2 tablespoons lemon juice
2 tablespoons fresh coriander

BAGHAAR (SEASONED OIL)
2 tablespoons oil
½ teaspoon white cumin seeds
6 diced red chillies
4 cloves garlic

2 fresh green chillies finely
   chopped, to garnish

Pick over and wash the lentils. Place in a large saucepan with
1 pint/600ml of the water and the chilli powder, curry leaves, ginger,
garlic and turmeric, cover and simmer for 20–25 minutes or until most
of the water has evaporated and the lentils are soft enough to be
mashed. Remove from the heat and mash, using either a wooden
masher or an ordinary steel potato masher.

Now add the salt, tomatoes, lemon juice, coriander and ½ pint/
300ml water, and cook over a medium heat for about 5 minutes,
stirring occasionally. Remove from the heat and set aside.

To make the *baghaar*, heat the oil and throw in all the spices. Wait
for about 30 seconds or until the spices turn a shade darker. Turn the
heat off and let the oil cool a little before pouring it over the lentils.

Serve garnished with chopped fresh green chillies.

Leek aur Chanay ki Dhaal

••

LEEKS AND LENTILS

T his spicy lentil dish is traditionally made with onion, but I use leeks to make it uniquely different. It is best served with chapati and any vegetable curry.

Serves 4
8 oz/225g *chana dhaal*
1½ pints/900ml water
2 leeks, washed and thinly sliced
5 tablespoons corn oil
4 tablespoons yogurt
½ teaspoon diced and crushed
   ginger root

½ teaspoon crushed garlic
½ teaspoon chilli powder
¼ teaspoon turmeric
1 teaspoon salt
1 teaspoon garam masala
¼ teaspoon black cumin seeds
2 tomatoes, sliced
2 tablespoons fresh coriander

Pick over and wash the lentils, and boil them in the water until they are soft. This will take about 30 minutes over a medium heat. Drain any excess water and set the lentils aside.

Fry the leeks in the oil until a soft golden brown. Meanwhile, pour the yogurt into a bowl and mix in all the spices and seasonings including the garam masala and black cumin seeds. Add this mixture to the leeks and stir-fry for about 2 minutes. Add the sliced tomatoes, fresh coriander and lentils and continue to cook over a medium heat for 3–5 minutes, stirring occasionally. Remove from the heat and let it stand for about 2 minutes for the flavours to blend before serving.

Chanay ki Dhaal aur Tamatar Methi

SPLIT PEAS WITH TOMATOES AND FENUGREEK

Fenugreek has a distinctive, extremely aromatic flavour unfamiliar to many people. Though I always recommend fresh fenugreek, it is available in its dried form if fresh is not easily obtainable. (It can also be frozen from fresh.) Fenugreek, fresh or dried, is obtainable from most Indian or Pakistani grocers. If using fresh fenugreek just pull the leaves off the stalk, avoiding any flowers as these can be bitter.

Serves 4

8 oz/225g *chana dhaal*, soaked overnight if possible

½ pint/100ml water

4 tablespoons corn oil

1 medium onion, peeled and chopped

½ teaspoon mixed onion and mustard seeds

2 curry leaves

2 tomatoes, sliced

½ teaspoon diced and crushed ginger root

½ teaspoon crushed garlic

1 teaspoon chilli powder

1 bunch fresh fenugreek leaves, *or* 1 tablespoon dried

1 teaspoon salt

2 tablespoons fresh coriander, washed and chopped

2 green chillies, finely chopped, deseeded if desired

Pick over and wash the *chana dhaal*. Soak it overnight if possible, and boil it in the water until it is soft but not mushy. Drain and set aside. Heat the oil in a saucepan and fry the onion until golden brown, then add the onion and mustard seeds and curry leaves. After a few seconds, add the sliced tomatoes, the ginger root, garlic and chilli powder, and stir-fry over a medium heat; then throw in the fenugreek leaves, *chana dhaal* and salt and stir-fry for about 1 minute. Add the fresh coriander and the chopped green chillies. Cover, lower the heat and cook for a further 5–7 minutes.

Serve hot with chapati or as an accompaniment to any of the curries.

Doodi aur Chanay ki Dhaal ka Salan

●●●

DOODI AND LENTIL CURRY

*L*ike many other fruit and vegetables, doodi *was not very easy to find in this country when we first came here, though now it is available in many good large supermarkets, where it is usually sold by the pound. This vegetable has a good texture and is delicious cooked this way. It can be served with Besun Ki Roti (page 114) as well as chapati, paratha or rice.*

Serves 4

3 oz/90g *chana dhaal*

1½ pints/900ml water

8 oz/225g *doodi*

4 tablespoons corn oil

2 medium onions, peeled and chopped

2 bay leaves

3 finely chopped green chillies, deseeded if desired

1 teaspoon ground cumin

¼ teaspoon turmeric

¼ teaspoon sugar

1 tablespoon lemon juice

2 tablespoons chopped fresh coriander

¼ pint/150ml water

Pick over and wash the *chana dhaal*, then boil it in the water until soft, drain and set aside. Wash, peel and thinly slice the *doodi*, cover with clingfilm and set aside. Heat the oil and fry the onions until golden brown. Add the remaining ingredients except the ¼ pt/150ml water, lower the heat and fry until the spices are well cooked. Throw in the *doodi* pieces and *chana dhaal*, and stir-fry for about a minute, or until the *doodi* has blended into the spices. Add the water, cover and simmer until the *doodi* is soft.

Serve garnished with more fresh coriander.

Toor Dhaal aur Tamatar

TOOR DHAAL WITH TOMATOES

Toor dhaal, *available from all Indian and Pakistani grocers, looks similar to* chana dhaal *but is a shade darker and is oily. Surprisingly, it is lighter when cooked. It cooks very quickly, so care must be taken not to make it mushy.*

Serves 4
4 oz/120g *toor dhaal*
5 tablespoons corn oil
2 medium onions, peeled and chopped
½ teaspoon mixed onion and mustard seeds
2 tablespoons chopped fresh coriander
½ teaspoon diced and crushed ginger root
½ teaspoon crushed garlic
½ teaspoon ground coriander
½ teaspoon ground cumin
½ teaspoon chilli powder
1 teaspoon salt
2 medium tomatoes, sliced
2 tablespoons lemon juice

Pick over and wash the *toor dhaal*. Boil until soft (about 15–20 minutes) and set aside. Heat the oil and fry the onions with the seeds until golden brown. Lower the heat and add the fresh coriander, the spices and salt. Add the *toor dhaal* and stir to mix well. Add the sliced tomatoes, cover and simmer for 3–5 minutes. Sprinkle with lemon juice and serve hot, garnished with fresh coriander if desired.

Sookhi Moong ki Dhaal

••

DRY MOONG DHAAL

*T*his dhaal *is a dry dish which would make a nice accompaniment to any curry which has a sauce. Serve with chapatis and* kachoomer *(page 104).*

Serves 4

4 tablespoons corn oil

1 medium onion, peeled and chopped

¼ teaspoon mustard seeds

¼ teaspoon onion seeds

8 oz/225g *moong dhaal*

½ teaspon diced and crushed ginger root

½ teaspoon crushed garlic

½ teaspoon chilli powder

½ teaspoon ground coriander

¼ teaspoon turmeric

1 teaspoon salt

1 tablespoon lemon juice

2 medium tomatoes, cut in wedges

2 tablespoons fresh coriander

1 whole green chilli, chopped

¼ pint/150ml water

Heat the oil in a deep frying pan and fry the onions and seeds until golden. In a separate bowl mix the ginger, garlic and ground spices along with the salt and lemon juice. Add this mixture to the onions and stir-fry for about 30 seconds.

Put the washed and picked-over *moong dhaal* into the onion mixture and mix it well. Add the tomatoes, fresh coriander and chopped green chilli. Pour in the water, lower the heat, cover and cook for about 12–15 minutes or until the lentils are soft but not mushy. If the lentils are not cooked add more water.

Masalay Dar Moong ki Dhaal

••

SPICED-UP MOONG DHAAL

*T*his *spicy vegetable lentil is one of my great favourites. You may if you prefer use* masoor dhaal, *but I like* moong dhaal. *It is good with both rice and chapati.*

Serves 4 as part of a meal
6 oz/180g *moong dhaal*
1 pint/600ml water
6 tablespoons corn oil
¼ teaspoon onion seeds
¼ teaspoon white cumin seeds
1 medium onion, peeled and
  sliced
5 dried red chillies
½ teaspoon diced and crushed
  ginger root
½ teaspoon crushed garlic

1 teaspoon chilli powder
1 teaspoon salt
1 medium potato, peeled and
  roughly cubed
4 oz/120g cauliflower, cut into
  small florets
3 oz/190g green beans, cut into
  1 in/2.5cm pieces
2 tablespoons fresh coriander,
  chopped
1 green chilli, finely chopped

Pick over, wash and boil the lentils until most of the water has evaporated and the lentils are soft but not mushy. Heat the oil and fry the seeds and onions until a nice golden brown. Throw in the red chillies and lower the heat before adding all the spices and vegetables, and cook for about 3–5 minutes. Now add the lentils and continue to cook, stirring, for a further 2 minutes. If the lentils get too dry add up to about ¼ pint/150ml of water.

Throw in the fresh coriander and green chilli, mix together and serve hot.

Sookhi Mili Huwi Subzee aur Dhaal

●●●

DRY MIXED VEGETABLES WITH LENTIL

I t is important that all the vegetables are finely chopped in this recipe, because they are cooked for a very short time. When preparing the cauliflower try to retain the floret shapes, so the cauliflower stays fairly crunchy. Serve wrapped in mini pooris (page 117) if desired, with kachoomer (page 104) as a side salad.

Serves 4

2 oz/160g *toor dhaal*
6 tablespoons corn oil
1 large onion, peeled and finely chopped
3 whole dried red chillies
½ teaspoon mixed mustard/onion/fenugreek seeds
3 whole curry leaves, fresh or dried
3 oz/90g aubergines, diced
4 oz/120g cauliflower, cut into small florets
5 oz/150g potatoes, peeled and diced
2 oz/160g red pepper, diced
2 or 3 green chillies, slit down the middle and deseeded if desired
¼–½ pint water/150–300ml water
1 teaspoon salt
1 tablespoon lemon juice
2 tablespoons fresh coriander

Pick over and wash the lentils, then boil them for about 10 minutes until soft. Drain and set aside. In a heavy-based saucepan heat the oil and fry the onions along with all the whole spices and curry leaves, stirring occasionally. When some bits of onion are darker than others, add the other vegetables. Lower the heat and carefully stir-fry for 7–10 minutes or until all the vegetables are cooked but still separate. Add the slit green chillies and the boiled lentils, mix everything together and add salt to taste. Sprinkle with lemon juice and fresh coriander, and continue to stir-fry for a further 2 minutes.

Serve hot.

Tarka Dhaal

●●

SEASONED LENTILS

I *use four different types of pulse for this* dhaal *dish, all of which are easily available from Indian and Pakistani grocers. A very versatile* dhaal *which will go with almost anything.*

Serves 4–6 as an accompaniment
2 oz/60g *moong dhaal*
2 oz/60g *masoor dhaal*
2 oz/60g *urid dhaal*
2 oz/60g *chana dhaal*
1 teaspoon crushed garlic
1 teaspoon ginger root, diced and
 crushed
1 teaspoon chilli powder
½ teaspoon garam masala

1 teaspoon turmeric
1½ pints/900ml water
1½ teaspoons salt

BAGHAAR (SEASONED OIL)
1 tablespoon corn oil
2 oz/60g unsalted butter
1 teaspoon white cumin seeds
1 medium onion, peeled and
 sliced
2 tablespoons fresh coriander

Pick over and wash the lentils at least twice, running your fingers through them. Place the lentils in a heavy-based saucepan, add all the spices (but not the salt), pour in the water and cook over a medium heat, half covered, for about 20 minutes or until most of the water has evaporated. Mash the lentils either with a wooden masher or by mixing them in a food processor for about 10 seconds. Remove from the processor and add the salt and more water if the lentils are too thick, and mix well. Transfer to a serving bowl and set aside.

To make the *baghaar*, heat the oil and butter together in a frying pan, throw in the cumin seeds, wait until these turn a shade darker and then add the onion and fresh coriander. Fry until the onions turn golden brown.

Pour the seasoned oil over the *dhaal* and serve hot.

Urid Dhaal

•••

URID LENTIL

U rid dhaal *is eaten most widely in the north of India. This is a very simple recipe and is a great favourite of my husband's. Serve it garnished with plenty of fresh coriander and green chillies and accompanied by freshly made chapati.*

Serves 4
6 oz/180g *urid dhaal*
½ teaspoon diced and crushed
   ginger root
½ teaspoon crushed garlic
3 green chillies, chopped
1 pint/600ml water
2 tablespoons fresh coriander
1 teaspoon salt

SEASONING
2 tablespoons oil
2 oz/60g butter
1 medium onion

GARNISH
2 tablespoons chopped fresh
   coriander
2 chopped green chillies

Pick over and wash the lentils two or three times or until the water is clear. Add the ginger, garlic, green chillies, water and fresh coriander and simmer over a low heat for about 25 minutes, or until the lentils are soft but not mushy and the water has been absorbed. Turn off the heat and stir in the salt. Dish up into a serving bowl.

In a frying pan, heat the oil and butter together and fry the chopped onion until golden brown. Pour the seasoning over the lentils in the bowl and garnish with the fresh coriander and chopped green chillies.

FISH AND SEAFOOD

Though most vegetarians, both in India and in Britain, will not even eat fish or eggs, many people who are vegetarians, for health reasons or otherwise, continue to eat seafood, and so I have included a few recipes here. Seafood is eaten all over India and Pakistan, and is particularly popular in certain parts of the Indian subcontinent, notably Bengal and around the city of Karachi. Indeed, the staple diet of the Bengalis is fish and rice; they enjoy river fish from the Hoogli and also lobster and king prawns, and they frequently use mustard oil when cooking it. Many of the recipes are prawn dishes; I recommend that you always use shelled prawns for curries as they absorb more of the spices in which they are cooked.

Tandoori Machli

TANDOORI-STYLE FISH

*T*his pleasantly spicy fish dish is traditionally cooked in a tandoor, a clay oven. Though ordinary cookers and grills can never repro-duce the effect of a tandoor, you can come pretty close by using a very hot grill that has been preheated for at least 20 minutes beforehand. By far the best method, however, is to cook it on a barbecue, in the open air. Serve with raita and a naan.

Serves 4
4 plaice fillets

MARINADE
6 tablespoons natural yogurt
3 tablespoons tomato purée
1 teaspoon ground cumin
1 teaspoon ground coriander
1 teaspoon crushed ginger
1 teaspoon chilli powder
1 teaspoon salt
1 teaspoon paprika

1 teaspoon crushed garlic
3 tablespoons fresh coriander, chopped
3 tablespoons lemon juice
2 tablespoons corn oil (optional)

GARNISH
4 lemon wedges
1 tablespoon fresh coriander
3 fresh green chillies, slit down the middle

Wash and trim the plaice fillets. Pat dry and set aside in a shallow ovenproof dish. In a separate bowl mix the ingredients for the marinade. Spread this mixture over the plaice fillets and set aside for about 1 hour. Preheat the grill for 20 minutes, until very hot, and place the fish dish under it. Keeping a close eye on the fish, grill for about 5 minutes, basting now and then with the spice mixture. If the fish looks a little dry, brush with 2 tablespoons of corn oil. Continue to grill for a further 10–12 minutes or until black burnt spots appear, for an authentic look.

Serve garnished with lemon wedges, fresh coriander and green chillies.

Masalay Dar Machli aur Dum ki Subzee

●●

SPICY FISH AND VEGETABLE BAKE

*T*his fish and vegetable bake is delicious served on its own or as part of a meal, with a crisp green salad.

Serves 4
1 lb/450g cod steaks

MARINADE
3 tablespoons lemon juice
½ teaspoon chilli powder
½ teaspoon ground ginger
½ teaspoon garlic powder
½ teaspoon garam masala
salt to taste

1½ lb/675g potatoes
4 tablespoons corn oil

1 medium onion, peeled and sliced
½ teaspoon onion seeds
2 medium courgettes, thinly sliced
2 medium tomatoes, diced
½ teaspoon chilli powder
½ teaspoon ground cumin
½ teaspoon ground coriander
2 tablespoons chopped fresh coriander
½ teaspoon salt
1 teaspoon lemon juice
8 oz/225g Cheddar cheese, grated

Wash and cut the cod into about 6 pieces. In a small bowl mix the ingredients for the marinade and pour over the cod pieces. Leave to marinate for about 1 hour. Meanwhile, peel, boil and mash the potatoes, and set aside. Preheat the oven to 400°F/200°C/Gas 6.

Heat the oil in a frying pan and fry the sliced onions along with the onion seeds. Gradually add the courgettes and tomatoes and the ground spices, and then the fresh coriander, salt and finally the lemon juice, and fry for about 5–7 minutes. Set aside.

Place the marinated cod under a preheated, hot grill for about 10–15 minutes, turning gently once. Arrange in an ovenproof dish and spoon the vegetable mixture over the top of the grilled cod pieces. Cover this with the mashed potato. Bake in the preheated oven for about 20 minutes.

Remove the dish from the oven and sprinkle on the grated cheese. Place under a hot grill until the cheese is melted and golden. Serve immediately.

Note Cod flakes rather easily when cooked, so be careful to use pieces of a reasonable size. Any firm-fleshed white fish can be substituted: you could try using haddock, monkfish or halibut.

Jhingay aur Tamatar

PRAWNS IN A CREAMY TOMATO CURRY SAUCE

I *prefer to use canned tomatoes for this as they help to make a better, thicker sauce. The fresh cream added at the end makes this delicately spiced curry fairly rich; yogurt may be used as an alternative. You may deseed the green chillies if you cannot take too hot a curry.*

Serves 4
10 oz/280g peeled prawns, fresh or frozen
½ teaspoon diced and crushed ginger root
½ teaspoon, crushed garlic
1 teaspoon chilli powder
½ teaspoon ground cumin
½ teaspoon ground coriander
1 teaspoon salt

14 oz/400g can of tomatoes, chopped
4 tablespoon corn oil
½ teaspoon mixed mustard and onion seeds
3 curry leaves
2 tablespoons fresh coriander, chopped, plus extra to garnish
2 green chillies, chopped
3 tablespoons single cream

If using frozen prawns, defrost these and leave in a bowl of cold water. In a bowl, mix together the spices with the chopped tomatoes. Heat the oil over a medium heat and when the oil is hot throw in the mustard and onion seeds and the curry leaves. Remove the pan from the heat and with a wooden spoon gradually add the tomato mixture. Stir-fry for about 7 minutes over a medium heat. Sprinkle over the fresh coriander and the chopped green chillies. Add the single cream and stir to mix. Turn off the heat.

Serve hot, garnished with sprigs of fresh coriander.

Jhingay Bharay Tamatar

TOMATOES STUFFED WITH PRAWNS

Y ou will need six firm beef tomatoes for this recipe, and most large supermarkets will have these, especially during the summer. Serve hot with a lentil dish or cold with salad.

Serves 6
6 large tomatoes
1 teaspoon crushed garlic
1 teaspoon chilli powder
½ teaspoon ground coriander
½ teaspoon salt
8 oz/225g peeled prawns

3 tablespoons corn oil
1 medium onion, peeled and finely chopped
½ green pepper, diced
1 teaspoon chopped fresh coriander

GARNISH
6 jumbo prawns
fresh coriander sprigs

Wash and dry the tomatoes. Carefully slice off the tops and remove the pulp with a spoon or grapefruit knife. Place the tomatoes in a greased ovenproof dish. Mix all the spices together with the prawns and set aside. Heat the oil in a frying pan and stir-fry the onion with the green pepper for about 1 minute. Now add the drained prawns and fresh coriander and cook over a low heat, stirring, for about 5–7 minutes. Leave the prawns to cool for about 5 minutes. Fill each tomato with a little of the prawn mixture, using a table- or dessertspoon. Place under a preheated hot grill for 10–12 minutes. Remove from the grill and garnish with the large prawns and sprigs of coriander.

Jhinga aur Kumbi Curry

CREAMY PRAWN AND MUSHROOM CURRY

A delicious combination of prawns and mushrooms in a light, creamy, mild sauce.

Serves 4

3 oz/90g unsalted butter
1 tablespoon corn oil
3 oz/90g onion, peeled and finely chopped
2 bay leaves
3 oz/90g peeled prawns
½ teaspoon garam masala

1 teaspoon black pepper
½ teaspoon salt
½ teaspoon ground coriander
¼ teaspoon turmeric
1 tablespoon Worcester sauce
3 oz/90g mushrooms, peeled and sliced
6 fl. oz/190ml fresh single cream

Melt the butter with the oil and fry the onion until golden brown. Add the bay leaves and fry for a further 1 minute. Add the prawns and all the spices and continue to stir-fry over a low heat. Add the sliced mushrooms and continue to fry for 5–7 minutes. Gradually add the cream and mix everything together, cover and leave to simmer for 5–7 minutes. Stir and serve.

Machli ka Salan

●●

FISH CURRY

F*or this fish recipe I try to use monkfish. Though expensive, it is a very firm-fleshed fish and will not break or fall to pieces easily. Cod or other firm white fish may also be used. The spicy tomato sauce makes this a very tangy, flavoursome dish.*

Serves 4
6 oz/180g monkfish (or other
   firm white fish)
3 tablespoons corn oil
1 large onion, peeled and
   chopped
1 teaspoon diced and crushed
   ginger root
1 teaspoon crushed garlic
½ teaspoon chilli powder
½ teaspoon salt
½ teaspoon ground coriander
¼ teaspoon mustard seeds
2 teaspoons lemon juice

2 tablespoons fresh coriander
2 tablespoons tomato puree
¾ pint/450ml water
2 fl. oz/60g single cream

MARINADE
1 teaspoon diced and crushed
   ginger root
1 teaspoon crushed garlic
½ teaspoon chilli powder
½ teaspoon salt
1 tablespoon fresh coriander
2 tablespoons oil
2 tablespoons lemon juice

Mix together the marinade ingredients and coat the fish fillets well. Leave to marinate for 30 minutes to an hour. Place under a preheated grill for 10–12 minutes, turning once and basting with oil.

Heat the oil in a saucepan and fry the finely chopped onion until golden brown. Add all the spices including the lemon juice, fresh coriander and tomato purée. Stir-fry for about 2 minutes over a low heat, add ½ pint/300ml water and cook until the water is absorbed. Add the remaining water and cook for a further minute. Add the cream, stirring continuously, then drop the fish pieces in and cook for a further 5 minutes over a low heat.

Gently transfer to a serving dish, trying not to break the fish pieces, especially if you are using cod.

Karahi Jhingay

••

KARAHI KING PRAWN

A karahi *is a utensil used in Indian cookery which is somewhat similar to the wok used in Chinese cookery. It is usually made of cast iron or stainless steel. Most Indian restaurants serve food directly from a mini version of a* karahi *at the table, which looks rather unusual and attractive. King prawns are best for this dish as they will stand out more than the ordinary kind; it makes a superb dinner party dish, accompanied by other vegetables and lentils. Try to use a* karahi *for this, but if you do not have one any thick, deep frying pan would do.*

Serves 4–6
5 tablespoons corn oil
2 medium onions, peeled and
  sliced
1 teaspoon crushed garlic
1 teaspoon salt
1 teaspoon chilli powder
½ teaspoon ground coriander

3 green chillies, deseeded and slit
  down the middle
1½ tablespoons fresh coriander
1 tablespoon tomato purée
1 green pepper, roughly sliced
12–14 king prawns, shelled
2 tomatoes, cut into wedges
1 tablespoon lemon juice

GARNISH
1½ tablespoons fresh coriander
4–6 lemon wedges

Heat the oil in a *karahi* and fry the onions until golden brown. Add the spices, green chillies and fresh coriander. Lower the heat and stir-fry for about 2 minutes so that the spices are well cooked with the onions. Now add the tomato purée, mix well and throw in the green pepper and the prawns. Cook, stirring, for 5–7 minutes, making sure that the prawns are well cooked. Add the tomato wedges and lemon juice, stir gently and cook for about 5 minutes, stirring occasionally. Remove from the heat.

Garnish with fresh coriander and lemon wedges, and serve hot and sizzling direct from the *karahi*.

Jhingay Masalay ki Pyaaz aur Macaroni

••

PRAWNS WITH SPICED ONIONS AND PASTA

I *always serve this creation of mine with Hara Masala Chawal (page 80) and any one of the raitas. It is not only a colourful combination but also a nourishing and substantial meal.*

Serves 4	1 teaspoon crushed garlic
6 oz/180g pasta shells	1 teaspoon chilli powder
5 tablespoons corn oil	1 teaspoon salt
¼ teaspoon onion seeds	6 oz/180g button mushrooms
4 curry leaves (optional)	8 oz/225g peeled prawns
2 medium onions, peeled and	2 green chillies, finely chopped
sliced	2 tablespoons fresh coriander

Boil the pasta shells in salted water until *al dente*, drain and set aside. Heat the oil and throw in the onion seeds and curry leaves, if using, wait for about 30 seconds and add the onions. Fry until golden brown. Add the garlic, chilli powder and salt, lower the heat and stir-fry the spices and onions for another minute. Throw in the mushrooms, pasta and prawns. Continue to stir-fry for a further 5–7 minutes.

Stir in the green chillies and fresh coriander and serve immediately.

Bhunay Huway Jhingay

•••

FRIED PRAWNS

I prefer to use king prawns for this dish but as these are expensive and not always easily available, ordinary frozen prawns will do as well. A little cream is added at the end to give it a thick creamy sauce, but yogurt could be used instead.

Serves 4–6 accompanied by
other curries
1 teaspoon chilli powder
1 teaspoon crushed garlic
1 teaspoon ginger root, diced
and crushed
1 teaspoon salt
½ teaspoon ground coriander
½ teaspoon ground cumin
1 tablespoon tomato purée

4 tablespoons corn oil
2 medium onions, peeled and
sliced
2 chopped green chillies
3 tablespoons chopped fresh
coriander, plus extra to garnish
12–14 king prawns, shelled, or
12 oz/340g small peeled
prawns
2 tablespoons fresh single cream

Combine the spices with the tomato purée and set aside. Heat the oil in a heavy-based saucepan and fry the onions over a medium heat until golden brown. Remove from the heat and, using a slotted spoon, remove the onions while leaving the oil in the saucepan. Place the onions in a food processor and process for about 30 seconds. Put the resulting paste back into the saucepan and return it to the heat. Now add the spice paste and stir-fry, adding the green chillies and fresh coriander. Add the prawns and continue stirring for about 2 minutes. Lower the heat and add the cream, cover and simmer for about 3 minutes, or until the prawns are cooked and well coated with the spices.

Serve garnished with more fresh coriander.

Jhingay ka Dopiaza

• •

KING PRAWN DOPIAZA

When the word dopiaza *is used it means that the dish is very oniony.*

Serves 4
5 tablespoons corn oil
3 medium onions, peeled and
 sliced
1 teaspoon ginger root, diced
 and crushed
1 teaspoon chilli powder
1 teaspoon crushed garlic

¼ teaspoon turmeric
1 teaspoon salt
½ red pepper, sliced
½ green pepper, sliced
2 tablespoons chopped fresh
 coriander
lemon juice to taste
10 king prawns shelled

Heat the oil in a saucepan until it is very hot, then add the onions and fry them until they are golden brown. Reduce the heat and gradually add all the spices, stir-fry for about 1 minute and add the red and green pepper. Throw in the fresh coriander and lemon juice to taste. Now add the king prawns and stir-fry gently, using a wooden spoon and scraping the bottom of the pan. Lower the heat, cover and cook for about 5 minutes, checking and stirring occasionally.

Serve hot with a chapati.

Masalay Dar Trout

●●

GRILLED SPICY TROUT

Beautiful fresh trout is easily available these days. Trout is delicious just grilled with a knob of butter, but this way of spicing it up is a truly mouthwatering way of eating it, and easy to do.
Serve with spiced potatoes (page 19) and a salad.

Serves 2
2 whole trout
1 tablespoon lemon juice
1 teaspoon ground cumin
1 teaspoon ground coriander
½ teaspoon powdered ginger

½ teaspoon chilli powder
1 teaspoon salt
1 tablespoon tomato purée
1 tablespoon fresh coriander
2 tablespoons corn oil

Top and tail the trout, wash and pat dry and sprinkle with lemon juice. Set aside. In a small mixing bowl, blend together all the spices and the salt with the tomato purée, fresh coriander and the oil.

Line a tray with foil and place the trout on it. Using a pastry brush, brush the trout on both sides with the spice mixture. Place under a preheated grill on medium heat for 10–15 minutes, turning once and brushing with any leftover spice mixture from time to time.

Machli aur Methi

•••

MONKFISH WITH CREAM AND FENUGREEK

I *find monkfish particularly good in curries as it has a firm texture and does not break up easily. Any other firm fish could be substituted.*

Serves 4 as part of a meal
1 lb/450g monkfish, cut into
   1 in/2.5cm pieces
4–5 tablespoons corn oil
2 medium onions, peeled and
   finely chopped
2 oz/60g fenugreek leaves
4 curry leaves
1 teaspoon chilli powder
½ teaspoon crushed garlic

½ teaspoon diced and crushed
   ginger root
¼ teaspoon turmeric
1 teaspoon salt
1 teaspoon creamed coconut
2 tablespoons fresh coriander
6 tablespoons fresh single cream
   or yogurt, *or* 3 tablespoons
   each of cream and yogurt

Heat the oil – preferably in a non-stick pan – and fry the fish pieces for 5–7 minutes, turning once gently. Remove the pieces and place on a plate. Fry the onions in the remaining oil along with the fenugreek and curry leaves. Add the spices, seasonings and creamed coconut and continue to fry for about 3–5 minutes over a low heat. Stir in the pieces of fish and the fresh coriander and cream or yogurt. Cover and heat through for 2 minutes before serving.

Machli kay Kebabs

●●

FISH KEBABS

*T*hese 'kebabs' are one of the nicest ways of eating fish: a soft spicy
fish mixture is fried until crisp and golden brown on the outside,
and served with tamatar methi (page 22) and chapati or any rice dish.

Serves 4
1 ½ lb/675g cod fillets
1 medium onion, peeled and
   finely chopped
1 teaspoon garam masala
1 teaspoon salt
1 teaspoon chilli powder
½ teaspoon ground *aamchoor*
   (mango powder)

½ teaspoon ginger root, diced
   and crushed
½ teaspoon crushed garlic
3 tablespoons chopped fresh
   coriander
2 green chillies, deseeded and
   finely chopped
2 eggs, beaten
6 oz/180g fresh breadcrumbs
oil for shallow frying
4 lemon wedges

Roughly cut up the cod fillets, place in a saucepan with a little water
and simmer gently for 1–2 minutes. Leave to stand in a sieve to drain
any excess water, and squeeze dry. Place in a large mixing bowl and
remove any small bones or skin. Add the onion and all the spices
including the fresh coriander and green chillies, and mix well to form a
fairly smooth consistency. Divide the mixture into about ten pieces,
making them into flat round shapes about ½ in/1cm thick.

Dip the fishcakes first into the egg and then into the breadcrumbs,
and shallow fry in hot oil, turning once. Drain on kitchen paper if
desired and serve immediately with lemon wedges.

RICE

There are so many different ways of cooking rice in India and it is such an important part of the diet and cuisine that I've included quite a few of my favourite rice dishes. Plain boiled rice is eaten every day with almost every meal, but for a more special meal rice is combined to delicious effect with spices and vegetables and/or meat and fish, to create pulaos and biryanis, which are particularly good in Hyderabad, where I come from.

I always use basmati rice because it is a good quality grain that gives excellent results, and I don't find it necessary to soak it before cooking, which is a time-saver. You can soak the rice if you wish — some people swear that soaking away the starch from the grains produces a better result. You can choose for yourself. Make sure you use a saucepan with a tight-fitting lid, and if necessary wrap the lid in tinfoil or a tea-towel to ensure a tight fit. Don't disturb the rice during cooking, and try not to lift the lid; if you have used the correct amount of liquid it should be safe to leave the rice on the heat for the time stated.

Before serving, gently stir the rice with a slotted spoon to incorporate air and fluff it up. You can keep it warm, covered, in a low oven, if necessary.

Nimboo kay Chawal

••

LEMON RICE

This delicate lemon rice is an original Parsee recipe. The Parsees, who came to India from Persia in the eighth century, introduced many Persian influences into Indian cooking, and though their cooking has become ingrained in Indian cooking their flavours and style are sometimes still quite distinct. This rice is very versatile and will go with almost any curry. It is especially good with the fish curry on page 63.

Serves 4
1 lb/450g basmati rice
4 oz/120g ghee *or* unsalted butter
2 oz/60g onion, peeled and sliced
½ teaspoon mustard seeds

1 teaspoon salt
¼ teaspoon turmeric
2 tablespoons lemon juice
1¼ pints/750ml water

Wash the rice thoroughly, drain and set aside. Heat the ghee and fry the sliced onions and the mustard seeds. Blend in the salt, turmeric, rice and lemon juice and mix everything together, gently stirring with a slotted spoon. Now pour in the water, lower the heat to medium–low, cover and simmer for about 20 minutes. Turn off the heat and allow the rice to stand for 5 minutes before serving.

Jhingay ka Pulao

●●

PRAWN PULAO

Pulaos can be fairly simple rice dishes, with the only additions being aromatic spices, or they can be main dishes containing fish, meat and vegetables. 'Pulao' in fact refers to the method of preparation: before cooking, the rice is fried with the spices and vegetables and other ingredients to make the finished dish flavoursome and spicy.

This Prawn Pulao is quick to prepare and makes a good centrepiece for a dinner party.

Serves 4

- 6 oz/180g peeled prawns, fresh or frozen and defrosted
- 1 lb/450g basmati rice
- 3 oz/90g unsalted butter
- 1 tablespoon corn oil
- 1 medium onion, peeled and chopped
- 1 teaspoon ginger root, diced and crushed
- 1 teaspoon crushed garlic
- 1 teaspoon chilli powder
- 1 ½ teaspoons salt
- 3 tablespoons lemon juice
- 3 tablespoons chopped fresh coriander
- 2 fresh green chillies, deseeded and finely chopped
- 1 ¼ pints/750ml water

Wash the prawns and place them in a bowl. Wash the rice and leave to soak for 30 minutes. Heat the butter with the oil (this prevents the butter burning) and fry the onion until golden brown. Add the spices and salt and fry over a low heat for about 1 minute, and then add the lemon juice, fresh coriander, green chillies and prawns. Drain the rice and add it to the prawn mixture, stirring it in with a slotted spoon. Add the water, bring to the boil, lower the heat to medium, cover and cook for 20–25 minutes. Turn off the heat.

Arrange in a shallow serving dish and serve immediately.

Kumbi Bhuttay ka Pulao

● ●

MUSHROOM AND CORN PULAO

O*nly whole spices are used for this unusual pulao rice.*

Serves 4
1 lb/450g basmati rice
2 oz/60g unsalted butter
1 tablespoon corn oil
1 medium onion, peeled and
  chopped
2 bay leaves

4 black peppercorns
3 green cardamoms
3 cloves
1 teaspoon salt
4 oz/120g mushrooms, sliced
4 oz/120g sweetcorn
1¼ pints/750ml water

Wash the rice, drain and set aside. Heat the butter with the oil (to prevent the butter burning), and fry the chopped onions until golden brown. Throw in the whole spices and salt and stir-fry for about 1 minute over a medium heat. Now add the rice, the mushrooms and the corn, and continue to stir-fry for a further 1 minute. Add the water and bring to the boil, cover and cook over a low heat for 20–25 minutes. When the steam begins to escape from the sides of the lid the rice should be ready. Let the rice stand for about 5 minutes before serving.

Jhingay aur Tamatar Pulao

••

PRAWN AND TOMATO PULAO

T*his prawn and tomato pulao is quick and easy to prepare.*

Serves 4–6
6 oz peeled prawns, fresh or
   frozen
1 lb/450g basmati rice
3 oz/90g unsalted butter
1 tablespoon oil
1 medium onion, peeled and
   sliced
1 teaspoon ginger root, diced and
   crushed
1 teaspoon crushed garlic
1 teaspoon chilli powder

1½ teaspoons salt
3 tablespoons lemon juice
2 tomatoes, sliced
3 tablespoons fresh coriander
1¼ pints/750ml water

GARNISH
4 lemon wedges
2 tomatoes, sliced
2 green chillies, finely chopped
2 king prawns

Defrost the prawns if necessary, wash them and set aside. Wash the rice and leave to soak for 30 minutes. Heat the butter and oil and fry the onion until golden brown. Lower the heat, add the spices and salt and stir-fry for about 2 minutes. Add the lemon juice, prawns, tomatoes and fresh coriander and stir-fry for a further 1 minute. Add the rice and mix everything together by stirring around gently. Add the water, bring to the boil, cover, lower the heat to medium and simmer for 20–25 minutes or until all the water has been absorbed and the rice is cooked. Let it stand for about 10 minutes. Gently separate the grains with a fork, and serve in a shallow oval dish, garnished with the lemon wedges, sliced tomatoes, green chillies and king prawns.

Moong Dhaal ki Khichri

RICE AND MOONG DHAAL

*A*khichri *is a dish where rice and lentils are combined. Simple to cook and delicious, it is usually served with either an egg curry or just a chutney and poppadums.*

Serves 4–6
12 oz/340g basmati rice
4 oz/120g *moong dhaal*
3 oz/90g unsalted butter
2 tablespoons corn oil
3 cloves
4 black peppercorns
4 green cardamoms

1 medium onion, peeled and
  chopped
¼ teaspoon turmeric
½ teaspoon diced and crushed
  ginger root
½ teaspoon crushed garlic
1 teaspoon salt
1¼ pints/750ml water

Wash the rice and lentils together and leave to soak. Meanwhile, in a heavy-based saucepan heat the butter and oil together, throw in the cloves, peppercorns and cardamoms, stir-fry for a few moments and then add the onions. Fry these for about 2 minutes, and then add the turmeric, ginger, garlic and salt. Add the lentils and rice and stir, using the *bhoon*ing method of quick, semicircular movements for about 1 minute to prevent them burning. Add the water, bring to the boil, lower the heat and cook for 20–25 minutes or until the steam begins to escape from the sides of the lid. Leave to stand for about 10 minutes to allow the rice to dry out. Mix and serve.

Subzee Pulao

••

VEGETABLE PULAO

This pulao is a complete meal and is ideal for strict vegetarians. You may use ghee, either vegetable or pure, or if you like, just use butter with a little oil (to prevent it burning).

Serves 4

- 1 lb/450g basmati rice
- 5 tablespoons ghee
- 2 medium onions, peeled and chopped
- 2 oz/60g carrots, peeled and sliced
- 2 oz/60g cut green beans
- 3 oz/90g sweetcorn
- 3 oz/90g frozen peas
- 1 teaspoon diced and crushed ginger root
- 1 teaspoon crushed garlic
- ¼ teaspoon turmeric
- 1½ teaspoons salt
- ½ teaspoon black cumin seeds
- 3 green cardamoms
- 4 tablespoons natural yogurt
- 2 tablespoons fresh coriander
- 2 tablespoons lemon juice
- 1 teaspoon garam masala
- 1¼ pints/750ml water
- 1 teaspoon saffron strands

Wash the rice and set aside. Heat the ghee in a medium saucepan and fry the onions until golden brown. Throw in the carrots, beans, corn and peas and fry for about 2 minutes. Add the remaining ingredients except the rice, water and saffron strands. Continue to stir-fry for a further 2 minutes or until the yogurty sauce thickens. Now add the rice, stirring it into the vegetables. Add the water and stir gently, using a slotted spoon. Now add the saffron strands. Bring to the boil, cover, lower the heat and cook for about 20 minutes or until all the water has been absorbed and the rice is cooked.

Leave to stand for about 10 minutes, mix and serve, decorated with halved hard-boiled eggs, if desired.

Subzee ki Biryani

••

VEGETABLE BIRYANI

A biryani is traditionally made by layering rice with vegetables and meat or fish – whatever you wish to use. It also contains the most expensive spice in the world – saffron – and usually yogurt. It forms a complete meal and is good served with a raita.

Serves 4

3 oz/90g cut green beans

3 oz/90g cauliflower, cut into small florets

2 oz/60g aubergine, diced

2 oz/60g carrots, sliced

3 oz/90g potatoes, peeled and diced

8 oz/225g ghee *or* unsalted butter

2 medium onions, peeled and sliced

5 black or green cardamoms

1 teaspoon black cumin seeds

4 black peppercorns

4 cloves

5 tablespoons natural yogurt

1 teaspoon diced and crushed ginger root

1 teaspoon crushed garlic

1½ teaspoons salt

½ teaspoon turmeric

½ teaspoon chilli powder

1 teaspoon garam masala

1¼ lb/570g basmati rice

2 tablespoons chopped fresh coriander

2 cinnamon sticks

1½ pints/900ml water

2 teaspoons saffron strands

¼ pint/150ml milk

2 teaspoons lemon juice

3 green chillies, deseeded and sliced

Wash and prepare all the vegetables and place in a bowl. Heat the ghee or butter in a large saucepan and fry the onions with three of the cardamoms, the cumin seeds, peppercorns and cloves until golden brown. Remove about a quarter of the onions and set aside. Add the vegetables to the pan and mix with the onions. Turn down the heat and, while the vegetables are cooking, mix the yogurt with the ginger, garlic, salt and ground spices. Slowly (so that it does not separate) blend the yogurt and spice mixture into the vegetables. Continue to stir-fry for a further 3 minutes. Turn off the heat and set aside.

Wash the basmati rice and place in a large saucepan with half the fresh coriander, the remaining two cardamoms and the cinnamon sticks. Add the water so that the rice is covered, bring to the boil, stir, and simmer for 10–15 minutes or until it is half cooked (you can check this by rubbing a few grains between your finger and thumb; each grain should still have a hard bit in the middle). Meanwhile, grind the saffron, add it to the milk and bring to the boil, and set this aside to infuse.

Spoon out half the rice into a large bowl. Place all the vegetables on top of the rice left in the saucepan and add half the remaining fresh coriander, one chopped green chilli and half the saffron and milk and the lemon juice. Place the remaining rice on top of the vegetables and add the rest of the fresh coriander, green chillies, saffron and milk and the reserved fried onion in ghee. Cover the saucepan with a tight-fitting lid (wrap foil around the lid if it is not tight fitting). Over a medium–low heat, cook the rice and vegetables for a further 20–25 minutes, or until the rice is done.

Allow it to stand for 5–7 minutes, and mix gently with a slotted spoon before serving.

Aloo Matar ki Tahari

••

POTATO AND PEA PULAO

T*his rice dish is delicious served with tomato and onion raita (page 105).*

Serves 4
1 lb/450g basmati rice
2 medium onions, peeled and sliced
5 tablespoons ghee (see page135) *or* unsalted butter
2 bay leaves
1 teaspoon ginger root, diced and crushed

1 teaspoon crushed garlic
½ teaspoon turmeric
6 oz/180g potatoes, peeled and cut into large dice
2 oz/60g peas
1¼ pints/750ml water
1 tablespoon chopped fresh coriander

Wash the rice and set aside. Fry the sliced onion in the ghee or butter until golden brown. Throw in the bay leaves and all the spices. Add the potatoes and peas and stir-fry over a low heat for about 2 minutes. Now add the drained rice and mix everything together. Pour in the water and throw in the fresh coriander. Lower the temperature and cook, covered, for 20–25 minutes or until the rice is cooked.

Serve hot with a refreshing raita.

Hara Masala Chawal

●●●

GREEN SPICED RICE

One of my favourite rice dishes because it is so versatile, this dish when cooked is a light shade of green, flecked with the whole spices.

Serves 4
1 lb/450g basmati rice
4 oz/120g ghee *or* unsalted butter
1 medium onion, peeled and
　sliced
¼ teaspoon onion seeds
¼ teaspoon mustard seeds
2 green chillies, deseeded if
　desired

½ teaspoon ginger root, diced
　and crushed
½ teaspoon garlic, diced and
　crushed
3 or 4 curry leaves
2 tablespoons fresh coriander
1 teaspoon salt
1¼ pints/750ml water

Wash the rice, drain and set aside. Once the ghee or butter is hot, throw in the sliced onions and the seeds. Fry until the onions are golden brown. Add the remaining herbs and spices along with the salt, lower the heat and stir-fry for about 1 minute. Add the rice, blend everything together and stir, scraping the bottom of the pan. Add the water and cover with a tightly fitting lid. Lower the heat and simmer for about 20–25 minutes or until the rice is cooked.

　　Serve hot.

Kabli Chana Pulao

•••

CHICK PEA PULAO

A lmost a meal in itself, this dish is delicious served with stir-fried vegetables.

Serves 4
1 lb/450g basmati rice
4–6 tablespoons corn oil
1 medium onion, peeled and
  finely chopped
½ teaspoon ground cumin
½ teaspoon ground coriander
½ teaspoon ginger root, diced
  and crushed

½ teaspoon crushed garlic
½ teaspoon chilli powder
½ teaspoon white cumin seeds
1 teaspoon salt
2 medium tomatoes, sliced
3 oz/90g cooked chick peas
1¼ pints/750ml water
1 tablespoon fresh coriander, to
  garnish

Wash the rice twice, drain and set aside. Heat the oil and fry the chopped onions until golden brown, lower the heat and add all the spices and salt. Add the sliced tomatoes, the chick peas and the rice, and stir-fry gently, mixing everything together. Pour in the water, cover and cook on a low heat for about 20 minutes. Allow to stand for 5 minutes.

Serve garnished with fresh coriander.

Subzee ki Khichri

•••

VEGETABLE KHICHRI

This khichri is a delicious variation on the simple rice and moong dhaal khichri on page 76 and, like the simple version, is quick and easy to prepare. I always prefer to use ghee or butter for rice dishes, but for health reasons you may wish to use corn oil.

Serves 4
1 oz/30g diced carrots
1 oz/30g frozen peas
1 oz/30g sweetcorn
1 oz/30g diced red pepper
1 lb/450g basmati rice
2 oz/60g *masoor dhaal*
1½ teaspoons salt
¼ teaspoon turmeric
½ teaspoon diced and crushed
   ginger root

½ teaspoon crushed garlic
4 oz/120g vegetable ghee *or*
   unsalted butter
1 medium onion, peeled and
   sliced
¼ teaspoon onion seeds
1 tablespoon chopped fresh
   coriander
2 green chillies, chopped and
   deseeded if desired
1¼ pints/750ml water

Prepare all the vegetables and wash and drain the rice and lentils. Set aside. Heat the ghee or butter in a heavy-based saucepan and fry the onions along with the onion seeds, fresh coriander and green chillies for about 1½–2 minutes. Throw in all the vegetables, lentils, salt and all the spices. Fry these over a medium heat for a further minute or so, scraping the bottom of the pan to prevent them sticking to it. Add the rice and fry for a further 30 seconds. Add the water, cover the pan with a tight-fitting lid and lower the heat. Cook for 20–25 minutes, or until the rice and lentils are cooked.

Let it stand for about 5 minutes and serve hot with a raita.

Tamatar ka Khana

●●●

TOMATO RICE

*T*his aromatic rice dish has an unusual colour and flavour, and is best served with okra and potato curry (page 13) and a tarka dhaal (page 55).

Serves 4
1 lb/450g basmati rice
4 tablespoons corn oil
4–6 fresh or dried curry leaves
¼ teaspoon onion seeds
¼ teaspoon mustard seeds

3 whole dried red chillies
1 tablespoon fresh coriander
1 teaspoon salt
3 medium tomatoes, sliced
1¼ pints/750ml water

Wash the rice, drain and set aside. Heat the oil in a saucepan and add the curry leaves, the onion and mustard seeds and the dried red chillies and fry for about 1 minute, reducing the heat. Now add the fresh coriander, salt and sliced tomatoes and stir everything together. Continue to fry for about 1½ minutes, scraping the bottom of the pan. Add the washed rice and stir everything well. Pour in the water, stir once more and cover the saucepan, bring to the boil, lower the heat and simmer the rice for about 20 minutes, or until the rice is cooked.

Allow to stand for about 5–7 minutes, and serve hot.

Tez Pattay kay Chawal

BAY RICE

S*erve this versatile, lightly flavoured rice with any of the firm curries and a lentil dish.*

Serves 4
1 lb/450g basmati rice
3 oz/90g ghee *or* unsalted butter
2 oz/60g onions, peeled and
   sliced
3 bay leaves

3 black peppercorns
2 green cardamoms
½ teaspoon caraway seeds
2 cloves
1 teaspoon salt
1¼ pints/750ml water

Wash and drain the rice. Heat the oil and fry the onions along with the spices over a medium heat until the onions are golden brown. Add the salt and rice and stir, using a slotted spoon so that the rice is not damaged. Pour in the water and bring to the boil, lower the heat, cover and cook for about 20 minutes or until the rice is cooked. Serve hot.

Gobi Pulao

●●

CAULIFLOWER PULAO

F or this recipe, cut the cauliflower florets fairly large so that they do
not break easily during cooking. The curry leaves may be omitted
here if you find them difficult to obtain.

Serves 4
1 lb/450g basmati rice
4–6 tablespoons corn oil
1 medium onion, peeled and
   sliced
½ teaspoon mixed onion and
   mustard seeds

3 fresh or dried curry leaves
1 teaspoon salt
4 oz/120g large cauliflower
   florets
1 tablespoon chopped fresh
   coriander
1¼ pints/750ml water

Wash and drain the rice. Heat the oil in a heavy-based saucepan and
fry the sliced onion until golden brown. Throw in the onion and
mustard seeds and the curry leaves and stir-fry for about 30 seconds.
Add the salt and the cauliflower florets, and fry for about 2 minutes
until golden brown. Add the rice and fresh coriander. Continue to
stir-fry for a further minute. Add the water, cover the saucepan with
a tight-fitting lid and simmer on a medium–low heat for about 20–25
minutes or until the rice is cooked.

Let it stand for about 5 minutes before serving.

Kumbi Pulao

••

MUSHROOM PULAO

I f you like mushrooms, you will love this delicately flavoured rice.
Serve it with any lentil dish and Miloni Subzee (page 37).

Serves 4
1 lb/450g basmati rice
1 tablespoon corn oil
3 oz/90g butter
1 medium onion, peeled and
  sliced
1 teaspoon onion seeds

1 teaspoon diced and crushed
  ginger root
1 teaspoon crushed garlic
1½ teaspoons salt
6 oz/180g mushrooms, peeled or
  wiped
1¼ pints/750ml water
1 tablespoon chopped fresh
  coriander to garnish

Wash the rice and leave to soak. Meanwhile heat the oil and butter and
sauté the onions until a soft golden brown. Throw in the onion seeds,
ginger, garlic and salt. Add the whole mushrooms and stir-fry for
about 2 minutes. Add the rice and stir, scraping the bottom of the pan.
Now add the water, bring to the boil, lower the heat, cover and simmer
for 20–25 minutes or until the water has been absorbed and the rice is
cooked. Leave to stand for 5–7 minutes to allow the rice to dry out a
little.

Serve garnished with fresh coriander.

Methi kay Chawal

●●●

FRESH FENUGREEK WITH RICE

This is a beautifully aromatic rice cooked with fresh fenugreek and a few spices. Fresh fenugreek is usually available all year round from Indian and Pakistani grocers. (Do not use the flowers as they can taste bitter.) Serve with any of the curries from this book and perhaps a lentil.

Serves 4
1 lb/450g basmati rice
4 oz/120g butter
1 tablespoon oil
1 medium onion, peeled and chopped
1 medium tomato, chopped
2 tablespoons chopped fresh fenugreek leaves

½ teaspoon mustard seeds
½ teaspoon diced and crushed ginger root
½ teaspoon crushed garlic
1 ½ teaspoons salt
1 ¼ pints/750ml water
3 hard-boiled eggs to garnish

Wash the rice and leave to soak for 30 minutes or so. Meanwhile, heat the butter and oil together, sauté the onions until soft and gradually add all the other ingredients, stirring and mixing everything together. Drain the rice and add it to the saucepan. Stir-fry for about 2 minutes. Add the water, bring to the boil, cover, lower the heat and cook for about 20–25 minutes or until the water is absorbed and steam begins to escape from the sides of the lid. When the rice is cooked, turn off the heat and leave to stand for 10 minutes.

Serve decorated with halved hard-boiled eggs.

SNACKS AND ACCOMPANIMENTS

I always feel that accompaniments do a lot for a simple meal. Most of them take very little time to prepare but add colour and variety, turning an ordinary meal into an interesting one. Most accompaniments should be made in small quantities as they are eaten in small amounts, as side dishes in the form of dips, relishes, salads and sauces.

Indian cuisine also includes a variety of snacks, like pakoras and dahi vadas, which are eaten off roadside stalls at any time of the day in India. These are all delicious served with either a chutney or some sort of mixed spice. Though people eat three meals a day in India and Pakistan, they still find they can eat snacks at tea-time, especially after a siesta in the afternoon.

The flours used for making the snacks can all be bought at Indian grocers. The most commonly used flour is wheat flour, also known as ata or chapati flour, but flours are also made from finely ground dhaals, such as gram flour, which is made from chana dhaal, and urid dhaal flour. Each has a distinctive flavour and texture.

Subzee ke Pakoray

••

PAKORAS

Pakoras are a delicious and very popular snack, rather similar to the better-known bhajis. These pakoras are particularly light, and are delicious served with a spicy tomato or tamarind sauce. Fresh fenugreek leaves should be picked off the stalks; do not pick off the flowers as well as these can taste bitter.

Serves 4

6 oz/180g onion, peeled and sliced

2 oz/60g potato, peeled and cut into matchsticks

2 tablespoons chopped fresh coriander

1 tablespoon fresh fenugreek leaves

1 teaspoon ginger root, diced and crushed

1 teaspoon crushed garlic

1½ teaspoons chilli powder

½ teaspoon cumin seeds

½ teaspoon salt

½ teaspoon baking powder

6 oz/180g gram flour (chick pea flour)

1 tablespoon oil

oil for deep frying

Prepare the onion and potatoes and set aside. In a small bowl blend all the spices together, including the coriander, fenugreek, garlic, cumin seeds, salt and baking powder. Pour this over the onion and potato mixture and add the gram flour, blending it in well with your fingers. Try and draw out as much moisture as possible from the onions. Use a little oil if necessary to moisten the mixture, and continue mixing until the mixture begins to stick together.

Heat the oil until hot in a deep frying pan. Drop about a dessert-spoonful of the mixture at a time into the hot oil and fry, turning the heat to medium to prevent burning. Turn once and remove from the pan when golden. Drain on kitchen paper.

Serve hot with a chutney.

Samosas

●●●

S amosas are triangular savoury pastries which are deep fried. Most
fillings are spicy mixtures of potatoes and other vegetables; in this
deliciously different version chana dhaal (split peas) are also included.

Serves 4 (Makes 8)

PASTRY
4 oz/100g self-raising flour
½ teaspoon salt
1½ oz/7.5g butter
4 tablespoons water

FILLING
1 lb/450g potatoes
4 tablespoons corn oil
1 teaspoon white cumin seeds
½ teaspoon onion seeds

6 oz/180g onion, peeled and
  finely chopped
1 teaspoon ground coriander
1 teaspoon garam masala
¼ teaspoon turmeric
½–1 teaspoon chilli powder
1½ teaspoons salt
2 oz/60g chopped fresh coriander
2 oz/60g *chana dhaal*, boiled
  until soft
3 tablespoons lemon juice
1 oz/30g cooked carrots and
  peas, chopped

Sift the flour and salt in a bowl. Add the butter, cut into small pieces,
and rub into the flour until the mixture resembles breadcrumbs. Pour
in the water, mix with a fork, pat the dough into a ball and knead with
the back of the hand for 5 minutes or until the dough is smooth. Add a
little flour if the dough is sticky. Cover and leave aside.

Peel, boil and mash the potatoes and set aside. Heat the oil in a
saucepan and add the cumin seeds, onion seeds and the finely chopped
onion. Fry over a medium heat until golden brown. Lower the heat and
add all the spices, salt and fresh coriander. Blend everything together
and remove from the heat. Pour this mixture over the potatoes. Add
the *chana dhaal*, lemon juice and mixed vegetables to the potatoes and
mix everything together. Leave to cool.

Break small balls off the dough and roll out very thinly into a circle.
Cut in half, dampen the edges and shape into cones. Fill the cones with
a little of the filling, dampen the top and bottom edges of the cones and
pinch together to seal. Set aside.

Fill a deep frying pan one-third full with oil and heat until a small
cube of stale bread turns golden in a few seconds when dropped into
the oil. Carefully lower the samosas into the oil a few at a time and fry
for 2–3 minutes or until golden brown. Remove from the oil and drain
on kitchen towels.

Masalay Dar Pyaaz kay Challay

•••

SPICY ONION RINGS

These spicy deep-fried onion rings are excellent served as an accompaniment to almost any meal. Though best served hot, straight from the pan, they are also delicious cold, and make a nice change for picnics.

Serves 4–6
4 tablespoons gram flour
½ teaspoon salt
½ pint/300ml water
½ teaspoon white cumin seeds
1 teaspoon chilli powder

½ teaspoon bicarbonate of soda
  or baking powder
1 tablespoon chopped fresh
  coriander
2 medium onions, peeled and
  sliced into rings
oil for deep frying

Sift the gram flour and salt into a bowl and add water to make a thick batter. Add the cumin seeds, chilli powder, bicarbonate of soda or baking powder and coriander, and mix everything together. Heat the oil in a deep frying pan. Drop the onion rings into the batter and, using a fork, transfer them to the hot oil. Fry until a crisp golden brown.

Place the rings on kitchen paper so that any excess oil is absorbed.

Note The oil for frying these rings should be *very* hot; otherwise the result will be soft and greasy.

Aloo Bonda

••

SPICY POTATO DUMPLINGS

Aloo Bonda *are surprisingly light, spicy potato dumplings deep-fried in a tasty batter. They can be served either as a snack at tea-time or as part of a vegetarian meal. If serving as a snack, allow 2 per person.*

Makes 10–12
3 medium potatoes, peeled
½ teaspoon coriander seeds, crushed
1 teaspoon crushed dried red chillies
2 tablespoons chopped fresh coriander
1 teaspoon salt
oil for deep frying

BATTER
6 oz/180g gram flour
½ teaspoon salt
½ teaspoon chilli powder
½ teaspoon crushed garlic
½ teaspoon diced and crushed ginger root
1 tablespoon chopped fresh coriander
½ pint/300ml water

Boil and mash the potatoes and combine with the crushed coriander seeds, dried red chillies, fresh coriander and salt.

To make the batter, sift the flour into a bowl, mix in all the other ingredients except the water and then gradually add all the water, beating to break up any balls that form. Make into a smooth paste. (You can do this easily in a food processor if you have one.)

Heat the oil in a deep frying pan. Make 8–10 small balls of the mashed potato mixture, about the size of golf balls, dip each ball into the batter and gently drop into the hot oil. Fry, turning the balls all the time, until they are a golden colour. Place on a kitchen paper to absorb any excess oil.

Serve immediately.

Bhel Poori

●●

O*ne of my favourite vegetarian snacks, this is a delicious and
    crunchy combination of poori (deep-fried bread) topped with
crunchy puffed rice, sev (tiny crispy gram-flour twists), potatoes and
chick peas. Served with a tangy tamarind chutney, it makes a mouthwatering snack or vegetable starter. You can buy the puffed rice and
sev from most Indian and Pakistani grocers.*

Serves 4

POORIS
3 oz/90g wheat flour *or chapati
    or ata* flour
2 oz/60g semolina
2 oz/60g plain flour
½ teaspoon salt
¼ pint/150ml water
oil for deep frying

TAMARIND CHUTNEY
2 tablespoons tamarind paste
2 tablespoons sugar
1 teaspoon salt

1 teaspoon chilli powder
¼ pint/150ml water

3 medium potatoes
4 oz/120g *sev*
4 oz/120g puffed rice
14 oz/400g cooked chick peas
2 tablespoons chopped fresh
    coriander
2 green chillies, deseeded and
    chopped
4 tablespoons natural yogurt
    mixed with 1 teaspoon sugar
1 teaspoon paprika

To make the pooris, sieve together the wheat flour, semolina, plain
flour and salt. Make a well in the middle, pour in the water and form
into a dough, adding more water if required. Knead for 2–3 minutes.
Cover and leave to stand for about 10 minutes. Break off pieces of the
dough about the size of golf balls and roll them out very thinly. Using
the cap of a jam jar press down on the dough to cut out about 15–18
small pooris. Heat the oil and deep fry these, turning once, until golden
and crisp. Drain on kitchen paper and set aside.

In a small bowl, mix together the tamarind chutney ingredients. Set
aside.

Peel and dice the potatoes into 1 in/2.5cm cubes, and simmer until
just soft. Drain.

To assemble the bhel poori, place the pooris on four small plates,
about three or four on each plate. Sprinkle half the *sev* and puffed rice
over the pooris. Top with the potatoes and the chick peas, distributing

them equally on each plate. Pour about 1 tablespoon of the tamarind chutney over each plate. Garnish with the fresh coriander and green chillies, and finish with about 1 teaspoon of the natural yogurt and a pinch of paprika over the top of each serving.

Bhoona Masala Bhutta

•••

SPICED BARBECUED CORN ON THE COB

S *picy barbecued corn on the cob is very popular in India and Pakistan, where it is most often sold and eaten by the roadside. Though corn on the cob is best barbecued over a naked flame, you can also use your grill, preheated to its highest temperature.*

Serves 6
6 corn on the cob, peeled and
    wiped clean
1 teaspoon chilli powder

1 teaspoon salt
3 tablespoons lemon juice
3 oz butter
2 lemons, cut into 12 wedges

Prepare the corn on the cob and set aside. Preheat the grill if you are using it. In a small bowl mix together the chilli powder, salt and lemon juice. Melt the butter and add this to the mixture. Using a pastry brush, brush each corn on the cob with the spice mixture and grill them, turning occasionally, and basting with more spice mixture. Serve each one with two lemon wedges. Continue until you have grilled or barbecued all the corn on the cob.

Dahi Vada (northern style)

LENTIL DUMPLINGS IN A YOGURT SAUCE

D*ahi vada are succulent lentil dumplings served in yogurt sauce (dahi means yogurt, and vada means dumplings). They are eaten as a snack or as part of a meal, or as party food. This version is widely eaten in the north of India and is sprinkled with either a sweet/sour-tasting tamarind sauce or a masala (a blend of black salt and whole roasted spices). I have included recipes for both, but it is entirely a matter of preference as both are quite delicious. The dumplings should be eaten at room temperature.*

Serves 4–6

DUMPLINGS
6 oz/180g *urid dhaal* flour
½ teaspoon ground ginger
1 teaspoon baking powder
½ pint/300ml water
oil for deep frying

YOGURT SAUCE
16 oz/450g yogurt
4 fl. oz/125ml water
2 tablespoons sugar
1 teaspoon salt

In a bowl, mix together the sauce ingredients and set aside.

In another bowl, mix together the ingredients for the dumplings, whipping them lightly until they form a paste. Heat the oil in a deep frying pan and drop teaspoons of this batter into the hot oil. Turn the dumplings over once and fry until golden brown. Drain on kitchen paper. Drop the dumplings into the prepared yogurt sauce and set aside to cool.

Make either the tamarind sauce or the masala (see below), whichever you prefer.

To serve, arrange the dumplings and yogurt sauce on a serving dish, and spoon or sprinkle over the tamarind sauce or masala.

IMLI KI CHUTNEY
TAMARIND SAUCE

2 tablespoons tamarind paste
5 tablespoons water
1 teaspoon chilli powder
½ teaspoon ground ginger

½ teaspoon salt
3 teaspoons sugar
1 tablespoon chopped fresh
 coriander

Place all the ingredients in a bowl and mix them together until you have a smooth paste-like consistency. If it is too sour for your taste, add more sugar. Just before serving, spoon the sauce over the dahi vadas.

MASALA

2 tablespoons coriander seeds   1 tablespoon crushed red chillies
2 tablespoons white cumin seeds   2 tablespoons citric acid
2 tablespoons black salt

Roast the coriander seeds and the white cumin seeds in a saucepan until they darken a little. Grind coarsely in a food processor or pestle and mortar. Add the black salt, crushed red chillies and citric acid and blend together. Just before serving, sprinkle about 1 tablespoon of this masala all over the dahi vadas.

Thalay Huway Karalay
FRIED BITTER GOURD

B*itter gourds are a type of marrow and resemble courgettes. To remove most of their bitter taste they are sprinkled with salt before being cooked (see also page 24). This dish makes a good crispy accompaniment to almost any meal, but goes particularly well with a tangy or tomatoey dish.*

Serves 4–6   2 curry leaves
3 bitter gourds   2 green chillies, chopped
1 tablespoon salt   1 tablespoon poppy seeds
2 tablespoons corn oil   ¼ teaspoon salt

Wash and deseed the bitter gourds and cut them into thin ¼ in/5mm slices. Leave covered with the salt for 2 hours, to draw out most of their bitter juices. Wash thoroughly, pat dry and set aside. Heat the oil in a frying pan and fry the curry leaves and chopped green chillies. Throw in all the bitter gourd slices and fry until they turn a little crisp but not burnt. Sprinkle with poppy seeds and salt and serve.

Dahi Vada (southern style)

CHICK PEA DUMPLINGS IN A YOGURT SAUCE

This type of dahi vada is eaten mainly in the south of India, especially in Hyderabad, where it is eaten almost daily in most Muslim households in the holy month of Ramzan. These gram flour dumplings are slightly more substantial than the ones made with urid dhaal flour (page 96), and are spicier and more tangy. Before serving, a baghaar (seasoned oil dressing) is poured over them for added flavour.

Serves 4

YOGURT SAUCE
16 oz/450g natural yogurt
1 teaspoon salt
½ teaspoon chilli powder

DUMPLINGS
6 oz/180g gram flour (chick pea flour)
3 oz/90g onion, peeled and finely chopped
½ teaspoon ginger root, diced and crushed
½ teaspoon crushed garlic

½ teaspoon chilli powder
2 green chillies, chopped
2 tablespoons chopped fresh coriander
½ teaspoon salt
1 teaspoon baking powder
½ pint/300ml water
oil for deep frying
1 tablespoon chopped fresh coriander to garnish

BAGHAAR (SEASONED OIL)
2 tablespoons oil
½ teaspoon white cumin seeds
6 dried red chillies

To make the sauce, beat the yogurt, salt and chilli powder together and set aside.

Sift the gram flour into a large mixing bowl, add the other dry ingredients and blend everything together with your fingers. Pour in the water and stir to make a thick batter. Fill a large mixing bowl with cold water and set on one side. Heat the oil in a deep frying pan and drop teaspoonfuls of batter into the hot oil. Cook until golden, turning once, and then place the dumplings in the bowl of water (this will help make them softer and lighter). When all the dumplings are fried, remove them from the bowl of water, drain as much water as possible from them and drop them into the yogurt.

Heat the oil for the *baghaar* and fry the cumin seeds and dried red chillies for about 40 seconds.

To serve, arrange the dumplings and yogurt sauce in a suitable dish and pour over the hot seasoned oil. Garnish with the chopped coriander, and serve at room temperature.

Aloo Chaat

●●

POTATO CHAAT (SAUCE)

Diced potatoes and chickpeas are drizzled with a tangy sweet and sour tamarind sauce, and topped with yogurt and spices to make Aloo Chaat, one of my favourite snacks. It can also be served as part of a vegetarian meal or as a starter.

Serves 4
1 lb/450g potatoes
6 oz/180g chick peas, soaked
   overnight

SAUCE
6–8 tablespoons boiling water
2 teaspoons tamarind paste
½ teaspoon ground ginger

2 tablespoons sugar
½ teaspoon salt

3 oz/90g natural yogurt
½ teaspoon chilli powder
pinch ground coriander
pinch ground cumin
1 tablespoon chopped fresh
   coriander

Peel and boil the potatoes in salted water until tender. Boil the chick peas until cooked. Drain these and set aside. Make the sauce by adding boiling water to the remaining ingredients and stirring until smooth. Pour the sauce over the potatoes and chick peas. Whip the natural yogurt and pour over the top of the sauce.

To serve, sprinkle with the ground spices and chopped fresh coriander.

Tamatar ka Kut

• •

TOMATO KUT (SAUCE)

T his is a thick spicy tomato sauce which is a typical Hyderabadi curry and is served as an accompaniment. Decorate it with halved hard-boiled eggs.

Serves 4
6 tablespoons tomato purée
1 teaspoon ground cumin
1 teaspoon diced and crushed ginger root
1 teaspoon crushed garlic
1 teaspoon ground coriander
1 teaspoon salt
1 teaspoon chilli powder
4 tablespoons corn oil
¼ teaspoon onion seeds

¼ teaspoon mustard seeds
¼ teaspoon fenugreek seeds
4 dried red chillies
2 teaspoons fresh coriander
2 teaspoons lemon juice
6 oz/180g water

GARNISH
3 hard-boiled eggs, halved
2 tablespoons fresh coriander
2 green chillies, chopped

In a bowl, combine the tomato purée with the ground cumin, ginger, garlic, ground coriander, salt and chilli powder. Set aside.

Heat the oil in a saucepan and throw in all the whole seeds and dried red chillies. After a minute or so, lower the heat and add the tomato purée mixture. Stir-fry, and stir in the fresh coriander, lemon juice and water. Cook for about 10–12 minutes, stirring occasionally. Turn off the heat and pour into a warmed serving dish. Garnish with the hard-boiled eggs, fresh coriander and green chillies.

Bonga Mirch aur Pyaaz Salad

•••

PEPPER AND ONION SALAD

This attractive and colourful salad may be served as an extra accompaniment to almost any food.

Serves 4
1 green pepper, finely sliced
1 red pepper, finely sliced
1 medium onion, peeled and
  finely diced

2 tablespoons lemon juice
2 tablespoons fresh coriander
½ teaspoon salt
2 mint sprigs to garnish

Arrange the peppers alternately with the onion on a plate. Sprinkle with lemon juice, fresh coriander and salt, garnish with mint sprigs and serve.

Kabli Chana Salad

••

SPICY CHICK PEA SALAD

*C*hick pea salad is a welcome change from an ordinary salad: it has a good texture and the chick peas make it more filling than most salads.

Serves 4
3 medium tomatoes, chopped
1 bunch spring onions, topped
   and tailed and cut into
   ½in/1cm pieces
3 carrots, peeled and diced
½ Iceberg lettuce, chopped
½ cucumber, sliced

15 oz/430g chick peas, cooked
   and drained
mint leaves to garnish

DRESSING
2 cloves garlic
½–1 teaspoon salt
3 tablespoons lemon juice
½ teaspoon chilli powder
1 tablespoon olive oil

Wash and prepare all the vegetables and salads and place in a large glass bowl. To make the dressing, crush the cloves of garlic and place them in a small bowl, add the remaining ingredients and blend everything together. Mix the chick peas with the salad and sprinkle with the salad dressing just before serving.

Garnish with fresh mint leaves.

Mooli aur Rajma ka Salad

DAIKON AND RED KIDNEY BEAN SALAD

Daikon, also known as mooli (in Indian and Pakistani groceries) or white radish, is a fresh-tasting, slightly peppery vegetable resembling a smooth thin parsnip. Its flavour and crunchy texture go perfectly with the other crisp ingredients of this salad, which complement the soft texture of the kidney beans.

Serves 4
8 leaves Iceberg lettuce
10 onion rings
8 oz/225g *mooli*, peeled and
   thinly sliced
½ cucumber, sliced
3 medium carrots, peeled and
   sliced

2 medium tomatoes, sliced
½ teaspoon salt
4 oz/120g cooked kidney beans
½ teaspoon paprika
1 tablespoon lemon juice
6–8 lime wedges to garnish

Lay the washed and dried lettuce leaves on a shallow oval dish. Place half the onion rings over the lettuce, and the *mooli*, cucumber, carrots and tomatoes. Sprinkle half the salt over the top. Spoon over the red kidney beans and arrange the remaining onion rings on top. Sprinkle on the remaining salt, the paprika and the lemon juice. Place the lime wedges around the dish, and serve.

Thill aur Kachoomer

●●

MIXED VEGETABLES AND SESAME SEEDS

This is an attractive-looking salad, especially if you can dice the vegetables equally. The roasted sesame seeds give this salad a crunchy texture. (Sesame seeds are widely available from health food shops as well as from Indian and Pakistani stores.)

Serves 4–6

3 oz/90g carrots, peeled, washed and diced into ¼in/5mm pieces

3 oz/90g cucumber, washed and diced into ¼ in/5mm pieces

2 oz/60g onion, peeled and chopped

2 oz/60g fresh coriander, chopped finely

3 oz/90g yellow pepper, washed and diced into ¼ in/5mm pieces

3 oz/90g tomato, washed and diced

2 oz/60g chick peas, cooked and drained

1 teaspoon salt

2 tablespoons lemon juice

1 oz/30g roasted sesame seeds

When you have prepared all the vegetables, toss them in an attractive salad bowl. Mix in the chick peas, sprinkle with salt and lemon juice and stir in. Now sprinkle the roasted sesame seeds over the top and serve.

Aloo ka Raita

• •

POTATO RAITA

R aita, a cooling and refreshing yogurty side dish for spicy curries, is
most frequently made with grated cucumber, but other vegetables
such as aubergine, tomato, potato or onion can be used for more
unusual raitas. Chopped mint and various spices may be added at the
last minute to give flavour and colour.

Serves 4–6
2 medium potatoes, peeled, sliced
   in ½ in/1cm pieces and boiled
   until soft but not mushy
10 oz/280g natural yogurt
2 tablespoons chopped fresh
   coriander

1 tablespoon chopped fresh mint
   leaves
2 green chillies, chopped
1 level teaspoon salt
½ teaspoon mixed ground
   cumin, ground coriander and
   paprika

Place the cooked cold potatoes in a serving dish. Whip the natural
yogurt and set aside. Mix together the fresh coriander, mint and green
chillies, and add them to the natural yogurt. Whip it all together with
the salt, and pour the yogurt over the top of the potatoes. Take two
large pinches of the mixed ground spices and sprinkle over the top of
the yogurt. Serve cold, with almost anything.

Kheera aur Pyaaz ka Raita

CUCUMBER AND ONION RAITA

This refreshing raita can be served as an accompaniment to almost any dish.

Serves 4
½ cucumber
2 oz/60g onion, peeled and finely
  chopped
½ teaspoon salt

2 tablespoons chopped fresh
  coriander
8 oz/225g thick natural yogurt
3 fl. oz/100ml water

Reserve about 5 thin slices of cucumber for garnish, and chop the rest finely. Place in a bowl with the onion, salt and coriander, and mix together. Whip the yogurt, mix with the water and pour over the cucumber and onion mixture.

Place in a serving dish and serve, garnished with the cucumber slices.

Podinay ki Chutney

MINT CHUTNEY

This versatile chutney goes with most curries and snacks. It should ideally be freshly made on the day of eating, but it can be kept in the fridge for 2 days.

Serves 4
1 medium onion, peeled and
   sliced
6 oz/180g fresh mint leaves
1 teaspoon sugar
1 teaspoon salt

2 green chillies, chopped
½ teaspoon garam masala
2 tablespoons lemon juice
1 teaspoon fresh coriander
mint leaves to garnish

Place the onions in a food processor and grind to a purée (this should take about 40 seconds), add the mint leaves and the remaining ingredients and mince these until they have blended together. Remove from the food processor and place in a small serving dish.

Garnish with a few mint leaves and serve.

Khatti Meeti Seb ki Chutney

SWEET AND SOUR APPLE CHUTNEY

Granny Smith apples' tart, crunchy qualities are best for this chutney. If you don't like your chutneys too tart add a little more sugar. Unless you know you like red chillies be careful about biting on them; they are very fierce!

Serves 4

4 tart eating apples	1 teaspoon salt
2 tablespoons oil	1 tablespoon lemon juice
1 teaspoon mixed mustard and	½ teaspoon shredded ginger
onion seeds	3–4 whole red chillies
	1 tablespoon sugar

Peel and roughly chop the apples. Heat the oil in a saucepan, throw in the mustard and onion seeds, wait until these begin to darken a little, then add the apples. Stir gently without mashing them. Add the salt, lemon juice, shredded ginger and the whole red chillies. Finally, sprinkle in the sugar and stir.

Remove from the heat and serve in a small chutney dish.

Kairi ki Chutney

GREEN MANGO CHUTNEY

This easy chutney is tart and hot; if you prefer milder chutney you could halve the number of green chillies.

Serves 4
2 large mangoes (kairi)
2 tablespoons lemon juice
3–4 green chillies, chopped
3 tablespoons chopped fresh coriander
1 teaspoon salt

Peel and remove the stones from the mangoes. Chop the flesh roughly and place in a food processor. Throw in all the other ingredients and process for about 40–50 seconds, stopping to stir if necessary. (Add a little water if needed to form a pulpy texture.) Taste for salt and hotness.

Spoon into a small chutney server and serve as an accompaniment to almost anything.

BREADS

Breads are important accompaniments to Indian meals. Ranging from plain, unleavened chapatis, which are generally used to mop up curries and sauces, to tasty, crispy poori, flaky rich stuffed parathas and the very popular naans, any number of breads are cooked daily in Indian and Pakistani households.

Many are made with finely ground wholemeal flour, called chapati flour or ata flour; you should be able to buy this from some supermarkets, or from Indian or Pakistani grocers.

In India, breads are often bought freshly made from roadside stands, or from restaurants (naans in particular, as these are made in tandoors or clay ovens which are not normally found in people's homes). I like to make my own breads and naans, which I cook under a very hot preheated grill, and I find them well worth the effort.

Most Indian breads freeze quite well. If you wish to freeze your bread, do so when you have formed the dough into individual portions. Thaw at room temperature and reheat either under a grill, in the oven, or in the microwave. Frozen breads cannot replace freshly made breads, though, and if time allows it is best to eat them directly they are made.

Naan

YEASTED FLAT BREAD

*M*ost *people back home buy naans from the local roadside baker,
where they are made in traditional* tandoors, *or eat them only
when they eat out. I realised I was not going to find such a convenient
supply of naan in England and decided to have a go at home. This
easy-to-follow recipe is the result. The sesame seeds give the naans a
crunchy, nutty outside. They are best served as soon as they are made.*

Makes 6–8
1 teaspoon fresh yeast
1 teaspoon sugar
4 oz/120g warm water
3 tablespoons natural yogurt

8 oz/225g plain flour
1 teaspoon salt
1 tablespoon ghee
2 oz/60g unsalted butter
1 teaspoon roasted sesame seeds

Put the yeast and sugar in a cup with the warm water and yogurt, mix
well until the yeast has dissolved and set aside in a warm place for 10
minutes, or until the mixture is frothy. Place the flour and salt in a large
mixing bowl, make a well in the middle, add the ghee and pour in the
yeast mixture. Mix well with your hands to form a dough, adding
more water if required. Turn on to a floured surface and knead for
about 5 minutes, or until smooth. Place the dough back in the bowl,
cover and leave to rise in a warm place for 1½ hours or until doubled
in size. Turn on to a floured surface and knead for a further 2 minutes.
Break off small balls with your hand and pat into rounds about
5 in/12cm in diameter and ½ in/1cm thick. Place on a greased sheet of
foil and grill under a very hot preheated grill for 7–10 minutes, turning
twice, brushing with butter and sprinkling with roasted sesame seeds.
    Serve warm immediately, or keep wrapped in foil until required.

Chapati

●●

UNLEAVENED BREAD

C hapati *are probably the best known of the Indian breads in the West. Chapatis are always circular, and measure about 6–7 in/15–17cm in diameter. No fat is used in making this bread, which is cooked on a thawa, a cast-iron flat pan or griddle with a handle, available from Indian or Pakistani stores. It is best to use a cloth, rolled up into a round shape, to move the chapati around on the thawa. In India chapati are cooked on a naked flame so that they puff up. Allow about 2 per person.*

Makes 8 (serves 4)   1 teaspoon salt
14 oz/400g wholemeal flour (*ata*)   ½ pint/300ml water

Sieve the flour into a deep bowl. Make a well in the middle, add the salt and water, and mix together to form a soft dough. Gather the dough from the sides of the bowl and knead until it is pliable, using the back of your fist. Cover and leave to stand for about 10 minutes. Divide into 8 pieces. Make each piece into a ball by rolling it between the palms of your hands. Dust each ball with flour to prevent the dough sticking, and roll out to form a circle approximately 6 in/15cm in diameter.

Heat the *thawa* to a very high temperature and place a chapati on it. Wait for about 10–15 seconds and turn the chapati over, pressing down with the cloth and moving the chapati around the *thawa*. Turn the chapati over again and repeat by moving the chapati around the *thawa*. After making sure that all the chapati and its edges are cooked, remove from the *thawa*. Repeat with the other chapati.

Like all Indian breads, it is best served as soon as possible after making. As they are cooked keep them warm, covered in foil, piled on top of each other. Brush each chapati with a little butter if desired, to help keep them moist.

Besun ki Roti

GRAM FLOUR BREAD

T*his unusual creamy-coloured bread is attractively flecked with green chillies and fresh coriander. It is a slightly more substantial bread than a chapati or a paratha.*

Makes 6 (serves 2–3)
4 oz/120g wholemeal flour
  (*chapati* or *ata* flour)
3 oz/90g gram flour
½ teaspoon salt
1 small onion, peeled and finely
  chopped

2 tablespoons finely chopped
  fresh coriander
3 green chillies, finely chopped
  and deseeded if desired
¼ pint/150ml water
2 teaspoons ghee

Sift the wholemeal and gram flours together into a large bowl. Stir in the salt, onion, fresh coriander and green chillies, and mix in the water. Knead to form a soft dough. Cover and set aside for 15 minutes. Knead for 5–7 minutes. Divide into 8 equal portions. On a lightly floured surface, roll them out to about 7 in/18cm in diameter, and cook over a medium heat in a heavy-based frying pan or a *thawa*, turning three times and lightly greasing each side with the ghee. Serve hot.

Paratha

••

LAYERED FLAKY BREAD

Parathas are thicker and slightly larger versions of chapatis, though they are crispy and more fattening as ghee is used to layer and fry them. You can use the same basic dough as for chapati, or, to make a softer dough, half milk and half water. Parathas can be made plain or stuffed with vegetables, meat or fish. I have included a recipe for cauliflower-stuffed paratha, but you can cook and use vegetables of your choice.

Makes 6 (serves 3)
14 oz/400g wholemeal flour (*ata*)
1 teaspoon salt
¼ pint/150ml milk
¼ pint/150ml water
5 tablespoons ghee

Sift the flour and salt into a deep bowl, and make a well in the middle. Gradually pour in the milk and water and mix the flour with your fingers until it forms a soft dough. Gather the dough from the sides of the bowl and knead until pliable, using the back of your fist. Cover and leave to stand for about 10 minutes.

Divide into 6 pieces and make each piece into a ball by rolling it between the palms of your hands. On a lightly floured surface, roll out into circles about 4 in/10cm in diameter. Spread about ¼ teaspoon of the ghee in the middle of each, using your fingers. Fold each one from the sides into the centre to make a 4 × 2 in/10 × 5cm flat piece, turn then fold in from both the sides again to make a square. Roll this out into a 7 in/17cm square. This will give you layers; the more layers you have the more crispy the bread will be.

Heat a heavy-based frying pan or *thawa* and place a paratha on it. Wait for about 10–20 seconds until bubbles begin to appear, then spread a teaspoon of the fat over the top. Turn over the paratha and quickly start moving it around using a flat spoon. Turn it again and move it around on the *thawa* until it is cooked. Remove and wrap in foil to keep warm. Repeat this with all the parathas.

Note it is best to use a *thawa* – a cast-iron flat pan like a griddle – for parathas, but a heavy cast-iron frying pan would do.

Gobi Bhara Paratha

CAULIFLOWER-STUFFED PARATHA

*T*his is a fairly rich and very tasty paratha, which can be eaten on its own as a meal, with apple chutney (page 108) or kachoomer (page 104).

Serves 4

3 tablespoons oil

3 curry leaves

4 oz/120g cauliflower, cut into tiny florets

¼ teaspoon diced and crushed ginger root

¼ teaspoon crushed garlic

½ teaspoon chilli powder

1 tablespoon chopped fresh coriander

1 green chilli, chopped

1 quantity paratha dough (page 115)

Heat the oil and fry the curry leaves until they turn a shade darker. Add the cauliflower florets and all the remaining flavourings, and fry until golden brown and tender. Using a masher, mash the cauliflower down, remove from the heat and place on kitchen paper to drain any excess oil.

Using the paratha dough, roll out two at a time. Spread about 1 tablespoon of cauliflower over one and place the other over the top. Fry in exactly the same way as for parathas (page 115), and serve warm with apple chutney or *kachoomer*.

Poori

●●

DEEP-FRIED BREAD PUFFS

A *poori is a deep-fried bread served mainly with vegetarian meals. The dough used is the same as that used for chapati, but pooris are deep-fried whereas a chapati is cooked on a* thawa *without fat. Once fried, the pooris should either be piled one on top of the other and wrapped in foil or left on a tray so that they remain puffed up. Allow two per person.*

Serves 5
8 oz/225g wholemeal flour (*ata*)
½ teaspoon salt

⅓ pint/200ml water
oil for deep frying

Place the wholemeal flour and salt in a bowl. Make a well in the middle, add the water gradually and work into a dough. Add more water if needed. Knead until smooth and elastic and set aside, covered, for about 15 minutes. Divide the dough into about 10 equal portions and with lightly oiled or floured hands pat each into a smooth ball. Roll out each ball thinly on a lightly oiled or floured surface into a circle about 6 in/15cm in diameter. Heat the oil in a deep frying pan or *karahi* and deep-fry the pooris, turning once, until puffed up and golden in colour. Remove from the pan and drain well.

Serve immediately if possible; otherwise, keep warm, wrapped in foil.

DESSERTS

Indian meals are usually concluded with something sweet, just as in the West. Fruit is often served — mangoes, guavas, custard apples — but for special occasions, rich, creamy and very sweet dishes are offered, such as rice or vermicelli puddings, ice-cream, bread pudding, and delectable sugary sweetmeats. Desserts are an often-neglected area of Indian cooking — but there is no reason for this to be so, as they are quite irresistible.

Chawal ki Kheer

••

RICE PUDDING

Rice pudding is a very popular dessert in India. It is cooked in a saucepan over a low heat, and is sweeter than the British version. On special occasions I decorate it with varq, the edible silver leaf. This rice pudding is flavoured with cardamoms and decorated with pistachio nuts and flaked almonds.

Serves 4
3 oz/190g basmati rice
2½ pints/1500ml milk
3 green cardamoms with husks removed and the seeds crushed
8 oz/225g white sugar

DECORATION
varq (optional)
1 oz/30g unsalted pistachio nuts
1 oz/30g flaked almonds

Wash the rice twice, add 1 pint/600ml of the milk and throw in the crushed cardamom seeds. Half cover the pan and cook over a low heat for about 20–25 minutes or until the rice is cooked and all the milk is absorbed, stirring occasionally. Remove from the heat and mash the rice down with a wooden masher. Mix in the sugar, pour in the remaining milk and return to the heat. Bring to the boil, stirring occasionally. Simmer gently until the pudding thickens and begins to coat the back of a spoon. (It should be the consistency of thick soup.)

Pour into a serving bowl and decorate with the *varq* if using, pistachio nuts and flaked almonds. Serve hot or cold.

Dhoodh Pawa

•••

FLAKED RICE PUDDING

Pawa *is flaked rice which is available at most Indian or Pakistani grocers and from some good supermarkets. This pudding contains a little rosewater for added aroma, but if you have difficulty obtaining this use a few drops of vanilla essence instead. This pudding may be prepared a day in advance as it is best served chilled.*

Serves 4–6
6 oz/180g *pawa* (flaked rice)
1¾ pints/1 litre full-fat milk
4 green cardamoms, with husks
   removed and the seeds crushed
8–10 tablespoons sugar
1 tablespoon rosewater

DECORATION
1 oz/30g unsalted pistachio nuts
1 oz/30g flaked almonds
pinch nutmeg
varq (optional)

Wash the *pawa* and set aside. Bring the milk to the boil over a medium heat with the cardamom seeds. Add the sugar and *pawa* and stir until the mixture is thick (about 10 minutes). Now add the rosewater, remove from the heat and transfer to a serving dish. Decorate with the pistachio nuts, almonds, nutmeg and *varq*, if using. Chill for about 2 hours before serving.

Tropical Fruit Salad

W hen we first came to England some 25 years ago, tropical fruit was hardly available. Nowadays, I am so pleased to see that fresh dates, mangoes, and the many different types of melons and pineapple are easily available. Though mangoes also come from South America and Africa, I always think that Indian and Pakistani mangoes are the most flavoursome and aromatic, and that if you haven't eaten one of those you haven't tasted a real mango. Serve this fruit salad with Greek yogurt or fresh cream.

Serves 4
1 Galia melon, skinned and diced
10 fresh dates, stoned and sliced
2 Indian mangoes, peeled and diced
1 lb/450g white grapes
4 slices pineapple, peeled and cubed
3 bananas, peeled and sliced
1 pomegranate, skinned
2 kiwi fruit, peeled and sliced
1 tablespoon caster sugar

When you have prepared all the fruit, place it in an attractive serving bowl and sprinkle with sugar.

Roti aur Anday ka Halva

●●

INDIAN BREAD PUDDING

*T*here is a traditional Indian bread pudding called Shahi Tukray, which does not contain any eggs, but I have changed the traditional recipe by using eggs and giving this pudding a custard base. It is delicious served hot or cold with fresh cream.

Serves 4–6
4 thin slices white bread
4 tablespoons ghee *or* 4
    tablespoons unsalted butter
    with 2 teaspoons oil
4 medium eggs
1¼ pints/750ml milk

8–10 oz/225–280g sugar
1 teaspoon saffron strands
2 oz/60g sultanas
2 oz/60g flaked almonds
1 oz/30g pistachio nuts, sliced
    (see page 125)

Preheat the oven to 400°F/200°C/Gas 6. Cut the crusts off the bread slices and cut each slice into 4 triangles. In a deep frying pan, heat the ghee or butter and oil (the oil prevents the butter from burning) and fry the slices over a medium heat, turning once so that the pieces are crisp and golden. Arrange these in a deep 8–10 in/20–25cm round dish and set aside. In a separate mixing bowl, beat the eggs, gradually adding the milk and sugar. Crush the saffron strands and add these as well. Pour this mixture over the bread slices, and decorate the top with the sultanas, almonds and sliced pistachio nuts. Place the dish in the preheated oven for 25–30 minutes, or until a knife pierced through the middle comes out clean. Remove from the oven and serve.

Gajar Bhatt

•••

CARROT AND RICE DESSERT

*C*arrots are used quite frequently in Indian cakes and desserts, and impart a sweet fresh flavour. Their most famous use in Indian cuisine is in the delicious sweetmeats Gajar ka Nelva. This satisfying pudding is good hot or cold and looks especially attractive served in a glass dish. The addition of a baghaar before serving adds a spicy flavour and aroma.

Serves 4
8 oz/225g basmati rice
12 fl. oz/360ml water
1 teaspoon saffron strands
3 oz/90g sultanas
8 oz/225g grated carrots
4 oz/120g pure ghee
4 fl. oz/120ml evaporated milk
10 oz/280g sugar

BAGHAAR (SEASONED OIL)
2 tablespoons pure ghee
4 whole cardamoms
3 cloves

GARNISH
3 oz/90g desiccated coconut
2 leaves *varq* (silver leaf)

Wash the rice, drain and place in a saucepan along with the water, saffron and sultanas. Bring to the boil, cover and simmer for about 15 minutes or until the rice is cooked. Transfer to a transparent serving dish. In a heavy-based saucepan, fry the grated carrots in ghee for about 5–7 minutes, stirring continuously. Add the evaporated milk and sugar and stir continuously for a further 2 minutes over a medium heat. Spread the carrot mixture over the rice mixture and, using a fork, mix the carrots into the rice. Prepare the *baghaar* by heating the ghee for about 1 minute in a heavy saucepan along with the whole cardamoms and cloves, and pour this over the dessert.

Serve hot or cold, decorated with the coconut and *varq* if desired.

Sevian

●●

FINE VERMICELLI CONDENSED MILK PUDDING

*I*ndian vermicelli (sevian) is very fine, and is available only at Indian
or Pakistani grocers. It is best to use it for this lovely rich creamy
dessert. Muslims traditionally eat this at the end of Ramzan, the holy
month. It is equally delicious eaten hot or cold.

Serves 4

1 oz/30g unsalted pistachio nuts
1 oz/30g flaked almonds
3 tablespoons ghee (pure or
  vegetable) *or* unsalted butter

6 oz/180g fine Indian vermicelli
  (*sevian*)
1½ pints/900ml milk
4 oz/120g condensed milk

Soak the pistachio nuts for about 2 hours to soften them, peel and slice
them and set aside with the flaked almonds. Heat the ghee in a deep,
heavy-based saucepan and fry the nuts until a shade darker. Remove
and place on kitchen paper. Now fry the vermicelli in the ghee, taking
great care not to burn them. Lower the heat and pour in the milk, turn
up the heat to medium and bring to the boil, and simmer for 5–7
minutes until the pudding is fairly thick. Now add the condensed milk
and continue cooking for about 5–7 minutes, stirring to prevent it
sticking to the bottom.

Taste for sweetness, pour into a serving dish and garnish with the
fried nuts.

Sevian ka Muzafir

•••

AROMATIC DRY VERMICELLI DESSERT

his sweet, saffrony dessert is made with khoya, *a thickened milk resembling cottage cheese, made by boiling and reducing a large quantity of milk. It might seem like quite a fiddle, but I assure you it is worth it for the rich, irresistible result. The more saffron you use the better. Serve with thick whipped cream.*

Serves 4–6

KHOYA (THICKENED MILK)
1 ½ pints/900ml milk

4 tablespoons pure ghee
10 oz/280g Indian vermicelli
   (*sevian*)
3 fl. oz/190ml evaporated milk

1 ½ teaspoons ground saffron
   strands
6 oz/180g sugar
¾ pint/450ml water

DECORATION
1 oz/30g flaked almonds
1 oz/30g unsalted pistachio nuts,
   boiled, peeled and slivered

To make the *khoya*, bring the milk to the boil in a large heavy saucepan, watching carefully. Lower the heat and simmer for 35–40 minutes, stirring occasionally, until the milk is reduced to a quarter of its volume. The milk should resemble a sticky, soft dough.

Heat the ghee in a heavy-based saucepan, and fry the vermicelli for about 1 minute, stirring continuously to prevent burning. Set aside. Blend the *khoya* with the evaporated milk and saffron and add to the vermicelli, return to the heat and stir around for a further minute. Transfer to a serving dish.

Boil the sugar and water together until reduced by almost half, and thick and syrupy. Pour this syrup over the *sevian* and serve hot, decorated with flaked almonds and slivered pistachio nuts.

Aam ki Kulfi

• •

MANGO KULFI

Kulfi *is a delicious ice-cream made with slowly evaporated milk rather than cream. Flavoured here with mango pulp, it makes an unusual dessert served with fresh peeled and sliced mangoes.*

Serves 4
3 pints/1800ml full-fat milk
6 oz/180g caster sugar

6 oz/180g mango pulp
mango slices to serve

Pour the milk into a heavy-based saucepan, bring to the boil, uncovered, and reduce the heat to medium. Leave the milk to boil, stirring occasionally to break the skin forming on top. Continue to do this until the milk is reduced to about a third of its original volume. Leave to cool, then add the sugar and mango pulp and blend everything well together. Pour the mixture into either 6–8 cone-shaped containers or a single plastic ice-cream container, cover tightly and place in the freezer. After about an hour return to the freezer with a spoon every 20 minutes and stir the mixture to break any ice crystals forming. Continue to do this until the *kulfi* is almost set. Remove from the freezer and leave at room temperature for 15–20 minutes to soften before serving with mango slices.

Pooran Puri

•••

HALVA IN PUFF PASTRY

*T*his *rather rich but delicious halva is a favourite recipe of mine, passed to me by my mother. It was made once a year in our house to celebrate a religious festival, and makes a delicious dessert or snack. If you don't want the trouble of making your own puff pastry, bought pastry will do equally well.*

Serves 6

PUFF PASTRY
2 lb/900g plain flour
1 teaspoon salt
1½ lb/675g firm unsalted butter
16–20 fl. oz/480–600ml ice-cold
  water

HALVA
10 oz/280g *chana dhaal*

1½ pints/900ml water
6 tablespoons ghee, pure or
  vegetable
3 green cardamoms, husks
  removed and seeds crushed
2 cloves
10 oz/280g sugar
3 oz/90g ground almonds
1 teaspoon saffron strands
2 oz/60g sultanas

First make the puff pastry. Sift the flour with the salt into a mixing bowl. Cut the butter into small pieces and drop them into the flour, coating them thoroughly with the flour. Add two-thirds of the water and form the flour into a dough, adding more water if necessary. Set the dough aside for about 15 minutes.

Now make the halva. Pick over the *chana dhaal* for any stones, and wash it twice. Place in a heavy-based saucepan with the water, half cover the pan and cook over a medium heat until all the water has evaporated and the *dhaal* is soft enough to be mashed into a paste. Using a food processor if you have one, mash the *dhaal* to a thick paste (you may need to add a little water). In a separate saucepan, heat the ghee and add the crushed cardamom seeds and cloves. Lower the heat and add the *chana dhaal* paste and start stirring and mixing, using the *bhoono*ing method (semicircular movements). Continue stirring, scraping the bottom of the pan, for about 5–7 minutes. Gradually fold in the sugar and ground almonds and continue bhoonoing for a further 10 minutes. Add the saffron and sultanas and blend together. By now the halva should have thickened and darkened in colour. Continue stirring for a further 3–5 minutes over a low heat. Remove from the heat and transfer to a serving dish.

Preheat the oven to 350°F/180°C/Gas 4. Place the pastry dough on a lightly floured board or clean surface and roll into a large square. Fold the pastry in three by turning the bottom third upwards and away from you and bringing the top portion down over it. Roll out once again and break the dough into three equal pieces. Roll out each one separately into a square, measuring about 8 × 8 in/20 × 20cm and ¼ in/15mm thick. Grease a tin or Pyrex dish and place one of the pastry squares in it. Spread over half the halva and place another rolled-out pastry square over the top. Now spread the remaining halva over this and place the third pastry square on top. Using a pastry brush, brush the top with milk. Bake in the preheated oven for 35–40 minutes.

Cut into squares and eat hot or cold.

Shakar Pare

••

SUGAR BITES

If you have a sweet tooth you will love this nutty, sticky Indian sweetmeat. It is easy to make and good to serve with tea or coffee.

Makes about 20
8 oz/225g water
6 oz/180g sugar
6 oz/180g plain flour
1 tablespoon ground almonds
2 oz/60g butter

2 tablespoons natural yogurt
½ teaspoon saffron strands, crushed
pure or vegetable ghee for deep frying

Boil the water and sugar together until thick (about 10–15 minutes).

Sift the flour into a large mixing bowl and add the ground almonds. Heat the butter until very hot and pour it over the flour and almonds. Whip the natural yogurt and stir it into the flour, along with the saffron. Gather the mixture from all around the bowl and form a dough. Knead it gently for about 2 minutes. Break off small balls of dough, about half the size of a golf ball, and place on a plate. Heat the ghee in a deep frying pan and drop in about 5 balls at a time. Deep fry until they turn golden, remove from the fat and drop into the syrup. Remove from the syrup and place on a serving plate, making sure they do not stick together.

URDU CHECKLIST

Titles of recipes are in most cases given in Urdu as well as English, and occasionally I use certain Urdu cookery terms such as *bhoono* and *baghaar* for convenience. The following checklist of such words will enable you to see at a glance what they mean.

aam mango
aamchoor mango powder
achaar pickle
akhrot walnut
aloo potato
anda egg
angoor grape
badaam almond
badi mirch green pepper
baghaar seasoned oil dressing
baingun aubergine
besun gram flour
bhindi okra (lady's fingers)
bhoono to stir-fry using semicircular movements, scraping the bottom of the pan
bhajia dumpling
bhujia vegetable curry
boti boned meat
bund gobi cabbage
chapati unleavened bread
chawal rice
chukander beetroot
dahi yogurt
dhaal lentils, pulses
dhania coriander
dum oven-cooked in its own juices

gajar carrot
goshth meat
halva sweet dessert
hara dhania fresh green coriander
hari mirch green chillis
jhinga prawn
kaddu pumpkin
kaju cashew nut
kela banana
khatti sour
kheema minced meat
kheera cucumber
khorma yogurt-based curry
khushka plain boiled rice
kisk-mish raisins
lassi yogurt-based drink
machli fish
makhan butter
masala spice
matar peas
mooli white radish
murgh chicken
naan yeasted bread
neembu lemon
palak spinach
paratha layered bread
phool gobi cauliflower

podina mint
poori puffed-up, deep-fried bread
pyaaz onions
raita yogurt-based sauce
roti bread
saag spinach
sabath whole
salan curry
seb apples

shakar kand sweet potato
shorwa sauce, gravy or curry
sooji semolina
sookhay (sookhi) dry
subzee vegetable
tamatar tomato
thalan fried
vada dumpling
zafran saffron

GLOSSARY

Aamchoor Sour-tasting mango powder made from dried raw mangoes. It is bought in jars.

Ata See **Wholemeal flour.**

Bay leaf (tez patta) One of the oldest herbs used in cookery, although not very widely used in curries.

Besun See **Gram flour.**

Bhoonay chanay Dried roasted chick peas, bought in packets.

Cardamom (elaichi) This spice, native to India, is considered the second most expensive (after saffron). The pods can be used with or without their husks and have a slightly pungent but very aromatic taste. They come in three varieties: green, white and black. The green and white pods can be used for both sweet and savoury dishes or to flavour rice, the black only for savoury dishes.

Cayenne pepper See **Chilli powder.**

Chana dhaal Very similar in appearance to moong dhaal – yellow split peas – this lentil has slightly less shiny grains. It is used as a binding agent and may be bought from Indian or Pakistani grocers.

Chana dhaal flour See **Gram flour.**

Chapati flour See **Wholemeal flour.**

Chilli powder (laal mirch) or cayenne pepper. A very fiery spice that should be used with caution.

Chillies, dried red (sabath sookhi laal mirch). These pods are extremely fiery and should be used with caution; their effect can be toned down slightly by removal of the seeds. Dried chillies are usually fried in oil before use.

Chillies, fresh green (hari mirch). Beautifully aromatic in flavour, these are used both in cooking and as a garnish. The seeds, which are the hottest part, may be removed if desired, by slitting the chilli down the middle. Never touch the face, especially the eyes or nose, while or after handling chillies: even after washing your hands will sting. Chillies are grown in Africa and Indonesia.

Cinnamon (dhalchini) One of the earliest known spices, this is grown mainly in Sri Lanka and has an aromatic and sweet flavour. It is sold both in powdered form and as sticks.

(laung) This spice is used to flavour many sweet and savoury dishes and is usually added whole. It is also sometimes used to seal a betel leaf for serving after an Indian meal (see paan).

Coconut (khopra or narial) Used to flavour both sweet and savoury dishes, fresh coconut can often be bought in supermarkets. Desiccated coconut and creamed coconut can also be bought and for most dishes make acceptable substitutes. Coconut is sometimes toasted for use in dishes (as for spices, see pages 4–5).

Coriander, fresh (hara dhania) This beautifully fragrant herb is used both in cooking and, finely chopped, sprinkled over dishes as a garnish.

Coriander seeds (dhania) This aromatic spice has a pungent, slightly lemony flavour. The seeds are used widely, either coarsely ground or powdered, in meat, fish and poultry dishes.

Corn oil Less fattening than any of the other oils, especially ghee, and also odourless, this is my preferred cooking oil.

Cumin, ground (safaid zeera) This musty-smelling ground spice is used widely, especially for flavouring lentils and vegetable curries. Its flavour improves upon roasting or frying.

Cumin seeds (shah zeera) Black cumin seeds, which have a strong aromatic flavour, are used to flavour curries and rice. White cumin may not be used as a substitute.

Curry leaves (kari patta) Similar in appearance to bay leaves but very different in flavour, these can be bought both fresh (occasionally) and dried. They are used to flavour lentil dishes and vegetable curries.

Fennel seeds (sonfe) Very similar looking to white cumin, these have a sweet taste and are used to flavour certain curries. They can also be chewed (as betelnut and cardamom are) after a spicy meal.

Fenugreek (methi) The flavour of the whole, dried, flat yellow seeds, a little bitter in taste, improves when they are lightly fried. Fresh fenugreek, sold in bunches, has very small leaves and is used to flavour both meat and vegetarian dishes.

Garam masala A mixture of spices which can either be made up at home from freshly ground spices or bought ready made. There is no set formula, but a typical mixture might include black cumin seeds, peppercorns, cloves, cinnamon and black cardamom. To make your own, grind together 4¼cm (1 in) cinnamon sticks, 3 cloves, 3 black peppercorns, 2 black cardamoms (with husks removed) and 2 teaspoons black cumin seeds. If desired, multiply the quantities, grind and store in an airtight jar for future use.

Garlic (lassun) This very useful spice is frequently used in curries, especially with ginger. It can be puréed in large quantities in a food processor and kept in an airtight container in the refrigerator. Whole cloves are sometimes added to lentil dishes.

Ghee (clarified butter) There are two types: pure (a dairy product) and vegetable. Though it was once a matter of pride to be able to claim that everything served in one's household was cooked in pure ghee, this is in fact quite high in cholesterol, so from the health standpoint it is better to use vegetable ghee or vegetable oil wherever possible (the majority of curries are cooked in oil). To make your own pure ghee melt 300g (8 oz) butter in a heavy saucepan and allow to simmer for 10–20 minutes. Once the milky white froth has turned golden, strain (preferably through muslin or cheesecloth) and store in a jar.

Ginger root (adrak) One of the most popular spices in India and also one of the oldest, this is an important ingredient in many curries and can be bought in good supermarkets. It should always be peeled before use and can be puréed in a food processor. Dried powdered ginger (*sontt*) is also useful to have in your larder.

Gram flour (besun) or *chana dhaal* flour (lentil flour) is used to make *pakoras* and is also used as a binding agent. A combination of gram flour and ordinary wholemeal flour makes a delicious Indian bread called *besun ki roti*.

Kevra water Iris water, used to flavour sweet dishes and sometimes rice. It is sold in small bottles.

Masoor dhaal Small, round and pale orange in colour, these split lentils are stocked by all supermarkets, labelled simply 'lentils' or 'red lentils'.

Moong dhaal This is a tear-drop-shaped yellow split lentil, more popular in northern India than in the south.

Mustard oil Often used in Bengali dishes, especially for cooking fish.

Mustard seeds (sarson ke beenji rai) These seeds, either black or yellow, are round and sharp-flavoured. They are used for flavouring curries and pickles.

Nutmeg (jaifal) The flavour of nutmeg, a native of Indonesia, is sweet and aromatic.

Onion seeds (kalongi) Black in colour and triangular in shape, these are used for both pickles and vegetable curries.

Paan Betel leaf dressed with calcium paste, fennel seeds, cardamom seeds, etc., wrapped and held together with a clove and sometimes covered with varq (edible silver leaf), for serving at the end of the evening to guests at an Indian party as a mouth-freshener. It may also contain tobacco, in which case it can be addictive. It can be bought or made at home.

Paprika This powder, made from dried sweet red pepper, is known as a hot-flavoured spice but is nothing like as hot as chilli pepper. Paprika is not used very often in Indian cookery.

Pepper Whenever possible use freshly ground black pepper if an Indian recipe stipulates pepper.

Pistachio nuts Widely used in Indian desserts, these are not the salty type sold in their shells but the shelled ones sold in packets at all Indian and Pakistani grocers.

Poppy seeds (khush khush) These dried whole seeds are always better when

... They are used, often whole, to flavour curries. Although they are ... the opium poppy, they do not contain opium.

Rosewater This is used mainly to flavour certain sweetmeats.

Saffron (zafran) This, the world's most expensive spice, is made from the stigmas of the saffron crocus, which is native to Asia Minor. Each 500g (1 lb) saffron needs 60,000 stigmas. Fortunately only a small quantity of saffron is needed to flavour or colour a dish, whether sweet or savoury. Saffron is sold both as strands and in powder form. It has a beautiful flavour and fragrance.

Sesame seeds (thill) Whole, flat, cream-coloured seeds, these are used to flavour some curries. When ground, they can be made into chutney.

Sev Very fine gram flour strands used in *bhel poori*, which can be bought in Indian and Pakistani grocers.

Tamarind (imli) The dried black pods of the tamarind plant, also known as the Indian date, grow freely in India and are sour tasting and very sticky. Tamarind has to be soaked in hot water to extract the flavour. Though it is much stronger than lemon, lemon is often used as a substitute. Nowadays tamarind can be bought in paste form in jars: mix with a little water to bring it to a runny consistency.

Turmeric (haldi) This bright yellow, bitter-tasting spice is sold ground. It is used mainly for colour rather than flavour.

Urid dhaal Though very similar in shape and size to *moong dhaal*, this one is white and a little drier when cooked. It is popular amongst northern Indians.

Urid dhaal flour This very fine white flour is used for *vadas* (deep-fried dumplings) which when soaked in yogurt make a delicious light snack, and for *dosas* (Indian rice pancakes).

Varq Edible silver leaf used for decoration purposes. It is very delicate and should be handled carefully. It can be bought in sheets from Indian or Pakistani grocers, but you may have to order it.

Wholemeal flour (ata) Also known as *chapati* flour, this may be bought at any Indian or Pakistani grocer's shop. It is used to make *chapatis*, *parathas* and *pooris*. Ordinary wholemeal flour may also be used for Indian breads, very well sieved.

INDEX